I0816930

GEOLOGY ENCYCLOPEDIAS

THE FOSSIL ENCYCLOPEDIA

BY MILES HERMAN

Encyclopedias

An Imprint of Abdo Reference

abdobooks.com

TABLE OF CONTENTS

ANCIENT LIFE ON EARTH

Fossils are the preserved remains and traces of organisms, or living things, that died a long time ago. To be considered a fossil, the remains must be at least 10,000 years old. Many fossils are millions of years old. Some have existed for almost four billion years. Paleontologists are scientists who study fossils. They help find and dig up fossilized remains. Fossils and scientific discoveries about them provide information about ancient life on Earth.

Fossils come in all shapes and sizes. Paleontologists divide fossils into two groups: body fossils and trace fossils. Body fossils are the fossilized remains of organisms such as plants, animals, and algae. They can also be parts of organisms, including bones, teeth, feathers, shells, and leaves. Body fossils help scientists figure out what organisms looked like. Trace fossils are marks or objects made by organisms. They show how organisms lived. Trace fossils include footprints, tail drags, and even poop. Some types of fossilized root systems may also be considered trace fossils of plants.

Fossils help show how Earth and its organisms developed. People have always been fascinated by fossils. For example, the ancient Greeks wrote about finding the fossils of shells and fish in dry areas. These remains showed that some lands were once covered by water. Today, people can see fossils at natural history museums around the world. These ancient remains continue to reveal the history of Earth.

Some fossils have been preserved where they were found. These include fossils found at the dig site Wadi Al-Hitan in Egypt.

HOW FOSSILS FORM

Since many fossils form underground, researchers must carefully unearth the remains without damaging them.

Most organisms do not become fossils after they die. They may be eaten by animals or broken down by bacteria and fungi. Eventually these organisms decay until no sign is left of them. Organisms need the right conditions to become fossils.

A common way that fossils are formed is when sediment covers an organism. Sediment is material left by water, wind, or glaciers. Dirt, sand, mud, and volcanic ash are types of sediment. A quick burial is best for preserving an organism.

The sediment protects organic matter from being eaten by scavengers. It also keeps out oxygen. Organisms that break down dead matter need oxygen to be efficient. The lack of oxygen slows down the process of decay.

WATER AND MINERALS

Fossils usually form in or near water. This is because water can carry large amounts of sediment that can cover an organism after it dies. New layers of sediment build up over time. The layers become heavier and harder. They compress, or squeeze together, to form sedimentary rock surrounding the dead organism.

Sedimentary rock can have tiny holes that let water reach the organism. The water contains minerals. These minerals fill in the open spaces of an organism or replace its tissue that has decomposed. The minerals harden over time, forming a fossil. This process is called permineralization. Once minerals replace all organic matter, the fossil is petrified. That means it has become rock. Over time, layers of sedimentary rock become exposed to the surface through natural processes such as erosion. This is the process through which wind, water, or other forces wear away rock. As rocks shift and erode, fossils emerge.

Mold and cast fossils are created when an organism leaves an imprint in sediment. Over time, the organism dissolves, but the imprint remains and hardens. This imprint is called a mold. Next, sediment and minerals fill the mold. They harden into the shape of the organism. This copied shape is called a cast.

AMBER AND TAR

Fossils can be formed in other ways too. Ancient organisms have been found in amber. Amber is the hardened resin of ancient trees. Resin is a thick, sticky substance produced by certain trees and other plants that hardens when exposed to air. It trapped small organisms long ago. Then the resin hardened.

Common amber fossils include spiders, flies, feathers, and even small frogs.

Resin sometimes preserves the organic material of an organism, such as its tissues. But under some conditions, such as the presence of moisture trapped in the resin, the organism breaks down. A trace or impression is left behind.

Other organisms were stuck in pools of a thick, black liquid called tar. Tar is produced by burned organic materials. Like amber, tar can preserve organisms. Scientists have found more than 600 ancient species fossilized in California's La Brea Tar Pits. These include mammoths and saber-toothed cats.

MUMMIFIED FOSSILS

Some fossils still have most of their soft parts. They are called mummies. Mummification usually happens in freezing or very dry conditions. Freezing temperatures can preserve animals, including their muscles, skin, and hair. The mummies of frozen mammoths have been found in icy places such as Yukon in northern Canada and other parts of the Arctic.

Mummies have been discovered in desert caves too. The dry conditions of these caves remove moisture from animals and preserve them. This drying process is known as desiccation.

LIVING FOSSILS

Living fossils are organisms that have stayed the same for millions of years. These species have evolved very little over time. They look almost the same as their ancient ancestors. Examples of living fossils include cockroaches, horseshoe crabs, and crocodiles. Plants such as the magnolia and monkey puzzle trees are also living fossils.

Tuatara are considered living fossils. They have existed in a similar form for 200 million years.

GEOLOGIC TIMESCALE

Earth formed more than 4.5 billion years ago. Geologists, scientists who study Earth, created a calendar to split up the massive amount of time since then. The geologic timescale is divided into eons, eras, periods, and epochs. Fossils from different times show how organisms have changed and evolved.

The Precambrian Era is a stretch of time that covers three eons. It reaches from Earth's formation to approximately 540 million years ago. Fossils from this time show very simple living organisms. In the Paleozoic Era, complex plants and marine animals began to evolve. Fossils from this era show some organisms slowly transitioning to life on land.

Dinosaurs evolved at the beginning of the Mesozoic Era. This era started about 252 million years ago. New species in this era also included mammals, flowering plants, and modern insects.

A mass extinction event 66 million years ago led to the disappearance of all dinosaurs, along with 80 percent of plant and animal species. This marked the end of the Mesozoic Era and the beginning of the Cenozoic Era. During this era, early primates and modern humans evolved. The Cenozoic Era stretches to the modern day.

Trilobites lived during the Paleozoic Era.

EON	ERA	PERIOD	EPOCH	MYA*
Phanerozoic	Cenozoic	Quaternary	Holocene	0.01
			Pleistocene	2.6
		Neogene	Pliocene	5.3
			Miocene	23.0
		Paleogene	Oligocene	33.9
			Eocene	56.0
			Paleocene	66.0
	Mesozoic	Cretaceous		145.0
		Jurassic		201.3
		Triassic		251.9
	Paleozoic	Permian		298.9
		Pennsylvanian		323.2
		Mississippian		358.9
		Devonian		419.2
		Silurian		443.8
		Ordovician		485.4
		Cambrian		541.0
Proterozoic	Precambrian			2500
Archean				4000
Hadean				4600

*Million Years Ago

PLANTS AND PLANT-LIKE ORGANISMS

Cutting a fossilized *Araucaria mirabilis* cone in half reveals its structure. Each scale contains a single seed that resembles a pine nut.

ARAUCARIA MIRABILIS

Araucaria mirabilis is an extinct conifer tree. Conifers are plants that bear their seeds in cones. Fossils of *A. mirabilis* date back about 230 million years.

Petrified cones are the size of lemons. Some cones were preserved after a volcano exploded and covered plants in ash. Rain and floods likely followed soon after. Minerals from the water seeped into the cones and hardened. Over time, these cones turned into a hard mineral called quartz.

A. mirabilis fossils can be found in Petrified Forest National Park in Argentina.

GIANT TREES

Almost all *A. mirabilis* fossils have been found in the Patagonia region of Argentina. The area is now a desert but was once a rainy forest. These fossils include petrified tree trunks. Some trunks were discovered standing where the trees had once grown. Scientists measured fossilized tree trunks to estimate the size of living *A. mirabilis* trees. *A. mirabilis* likely grew up to 328 feet (100 m) tall.

Fossils reveal that *Archaeopteris* reproduced through spores instead of seeds, similarly to modern ferns.

ARCHAEOPTERIS

Archaeopteris is known as the earliest modern tree. It lived 370 to 350 million years ago. This genus once filled 90 percent of the world's forests. It had a woody trunk. However, fossilized leaf impressions indicate that *Archaeopteris* had fern-like leaves, unlike those of trees today.

BRANCHING OUT

In the early 1990s, scientists discovered hundreds of new *Archaeopteris* fossils in Morocco. Many *Archaeopteris* populated lowlands near the ocean. These trees fell into the ocean and were buried under marine sediment. Today, the area is a desert.

Some trunk fossils showed points where *Archaeopteris* limbs branched out. *Archaeopteris* branches grew with wide bases to support their weight. This formation shows that even the earliest woody trees had the same basic branch structure as modern trees. The fossilized trunks were up to 3 feet (1 m) wide. *Archaeopteris* grew to an estimated 60 to 90 feet (18 to 27 m) tall.

Rings in fossilized *Archaeopteris* trunks show how the tree grew each year.

CALAMITES

Calamites is a genus of plants related to modern horsetails. Horsetails are reed-like plants. Stems from *Calamites* are commonly found fossils. Fossils show scars at the joints where branches were once attached. *Calamites* had leaves arranged in whorls.

Fossils show how the stem of *Calamites* was segmented. Each stem usually shows several sections that are separated by joints.

WETLAND PLANT

Calamites fossils have been found throughout the world. These fossils are found in sedimentary rocks. Many rocks are from wetlands. Based on the age and type of rock, *Calamites* likely grew during the Carboniferous Period, about 360 to 299 million years ago. It grew in sediment close to lakes and rivers. *Calamites* could grow up to 100 feet (30 m) tall. *Calamites* plants were much larger than modern horsetails, which range from 3 to 5 feet (1 to 1.5 m) tall.

Calamites fossils also include impressions left in rock.

Stems of *Calamites* were hollow. They were often preserved as cast fossils. Minerals in water entered the open space in the center of the stem and hardened.

Fossilized *Cladophlebis* fronds display a leaf-like structure. They show a long stem with leaflets branching off in pairs.

CLADOPHLEBIS

Cladophlebis was a fern that grew in abundance during the Jurassic Period. Ferns are plants that usually reproduce by spores, which are smaller and simpler than seeds. *Cladophlebis* fossils have been found in North America, New Zealand, and Australia. Many fossils are roots, stems, fronds, and spores. Fronds were about 2 feet (0.6 m) long. Many fossils are fragmented. They show only part of the plant.

TRACKING FERNS AND SPORES

Cladophlebis, like modern ferns, grew in difficult environments. Ferns are among the first plants to grow after forest fires and volcanic eruptions. Researchers have studied *Cladophlebis* fossils, including its spores, to track prehistoric catastrophes. A large collection of *Cladophlebis* spore fossils tells scientists that a natural disaster may have occurred at about the same time the fossils were formed.

COCCOLITHS

Coccoliths are scales that cover coccolithophores, a type of marine algae. Each coccolithophore has at least 30 scales. The scales are made from calcite, a mineral that forms rocks. Coccoliths are microscopic fossils that first developed 542 to 488 million years ago. It would take more than one million coccoliths to cover a penny. Coccolithophores still grow today.

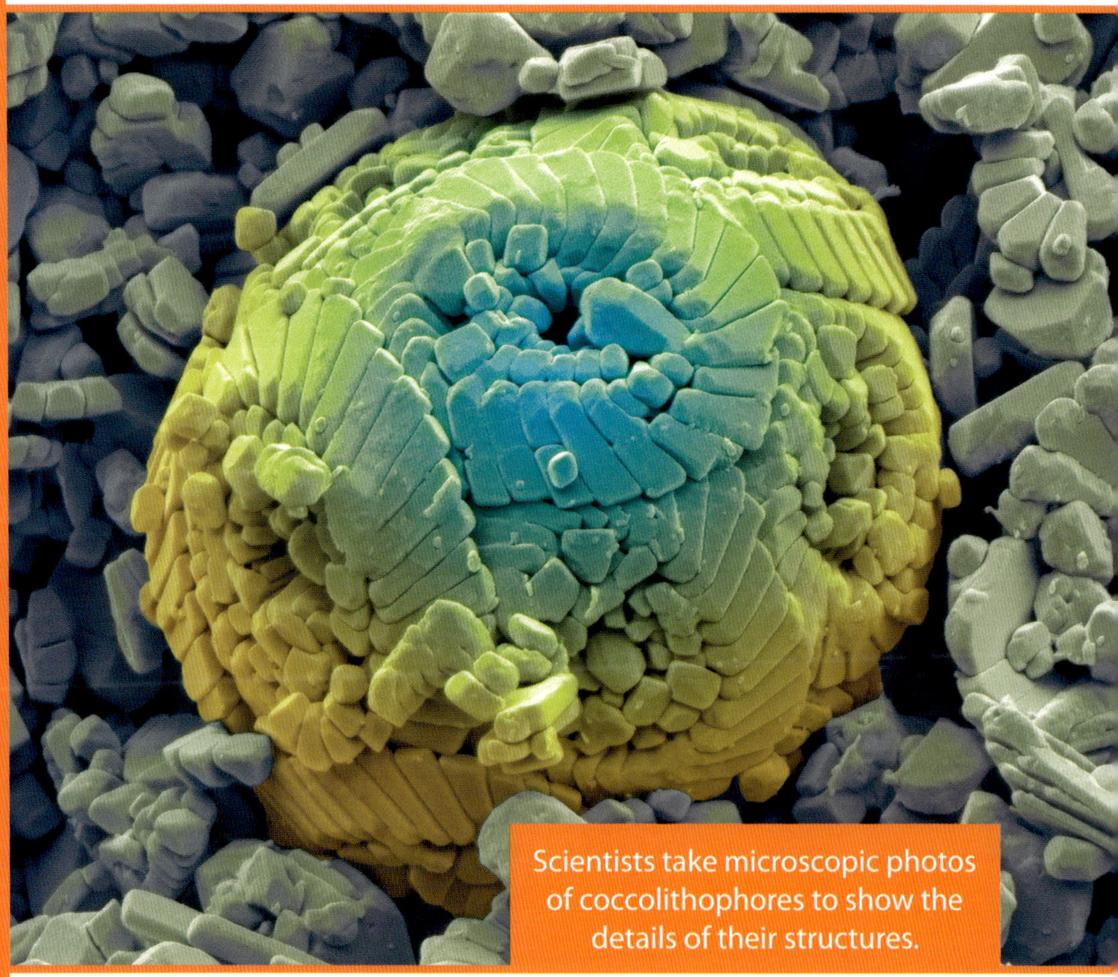

Scientists take microscopic photos of coccolithophores to show the details of their structures.

The White Cliffs of Dover in England are a famous example of a formation made from coccolith-rich chalk.

CHALK

Fossilized coccoliths are often found in chalk, a soft rock. All chalk is made from the shells or scales of microscopic marine organisms such as coccolithophores. The formation of chalk starts when coccoliths sink to the ocean floor. Sand covers them and compacts over millions of years. The movement of Earth's crust caused some deposits to rise above sea level.

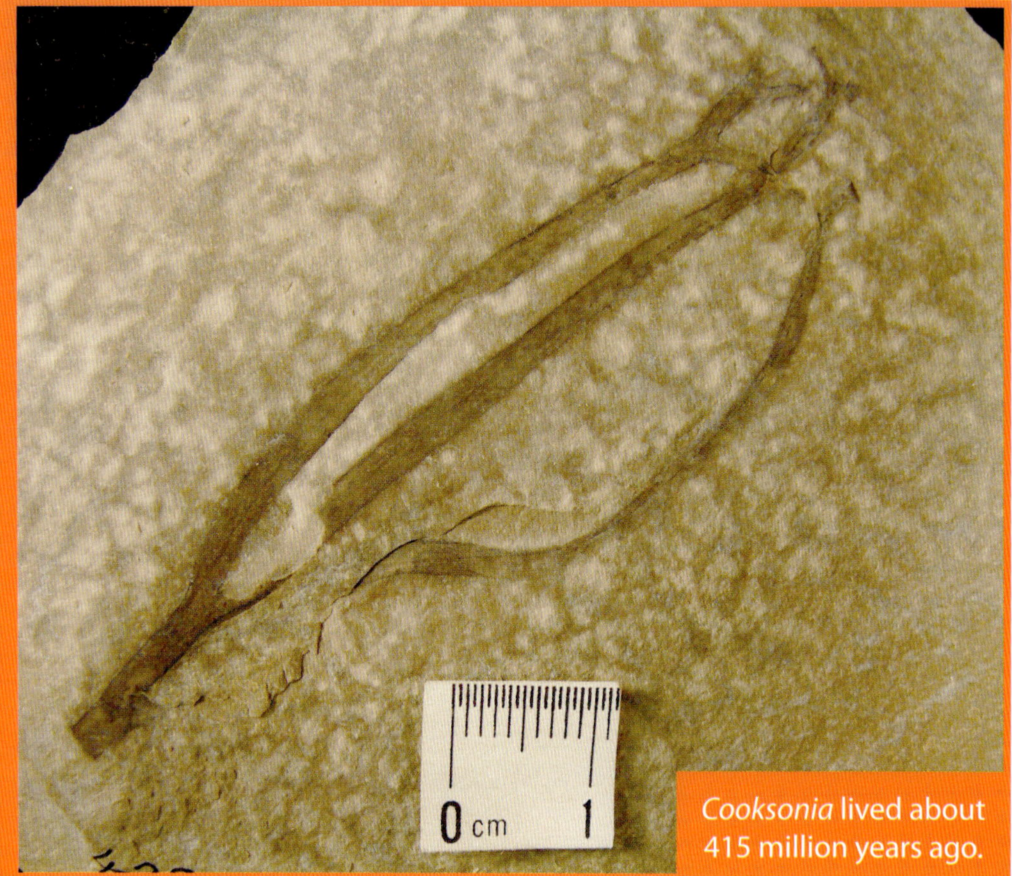

Cooksonia lived about 415 million years ago.

COOKSONIA

Cooksonia was one of the first vascular plants able to thrive on land. Vascular plants have special tissues that move water and minerals through the organism. *Cooksonia* lived on shores near lakes and rivers throughout the world during the Paleozoic Era.

Many fossils of *Cooksonia* show a simple structure. The plant did not have leaves, roots, seeds, or flowers. Instead, it had a Y-branching stem that ended in spore sacs. These sacs are called sporangia. *Cooksonia* was likely less than 4 inches (10 cm) tall. But many fossils are even smaller. This is because part of the stem is missing.

PIONEERING BOTANIST

Botanist W. H. Lang discovered the first *Cooksonia* fossil in a Welsh quarry. Experts thought it might be a marine animal. But Lang saw spores in the fossil that showed it was a plant. Then he proved that it grew on land. He did this with a detailed study of the rocks where the *Cooksonia* fossil was found. It was discovered next to other Paleozoic land plants and animals. These nearby fossils showed Lang the age and habitat of *Cooksonia*. Lang first published his findings in 1937.

Fossils show the sporangia of *Cooksonia* flaring out in a trumpet shape. Artists have imagined what the living plant may have looked like.

EUPHORBIOTHECA DECCANENSIS

Euphorbiotheca deccanensis was a plant with small fruit that grew during the Mesozoic Era. The petrified fossils of the fruit are usually 0.15 to 0.2 inches (0.4 to 0.5 cm) in diameter. When cut in half, three chambers are revealed. Each chamber contains a single seed. When the fruit ripened, it dried out.

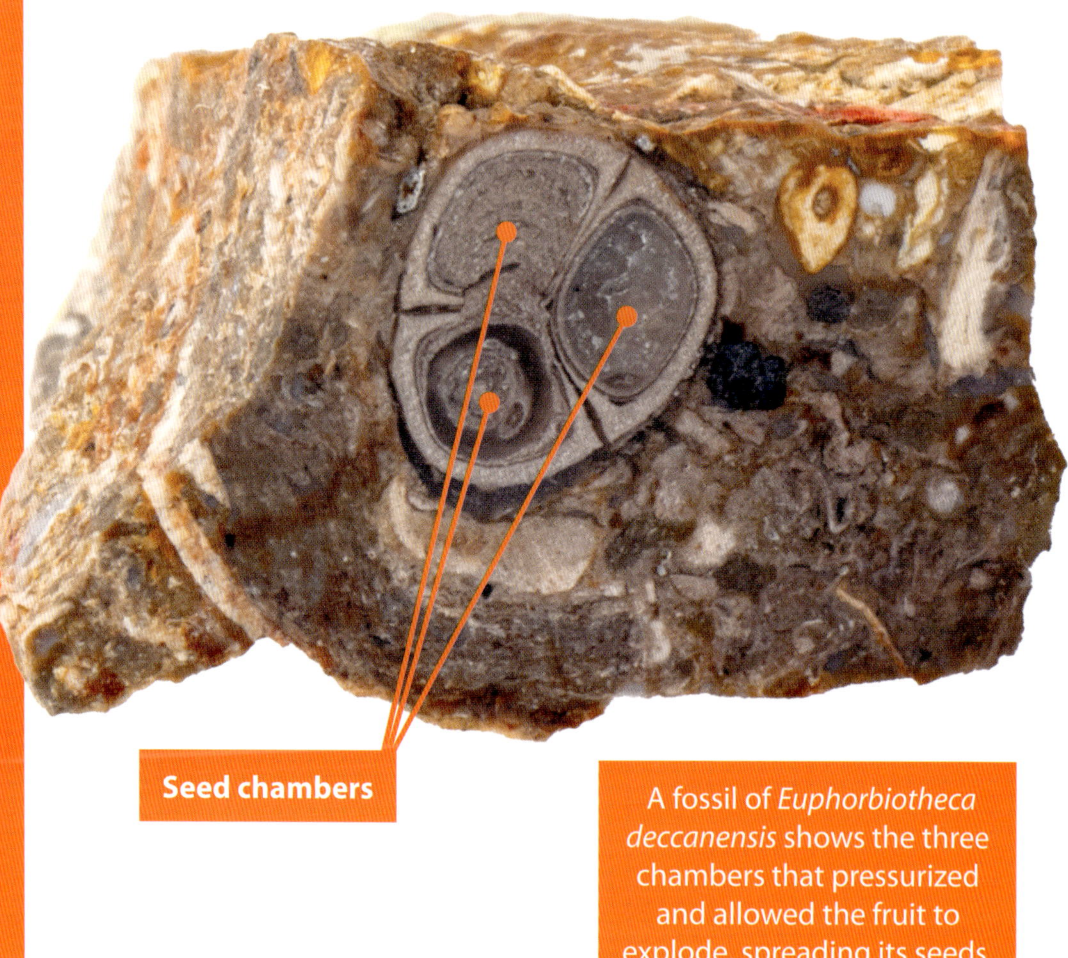

A fossil of *Euphorbiotheca deccanensis* shows the three chambers that pressurized and allowed the fruit to explode, spreading its seeds.

Modern sandbox trees have seed pods, *pictured*, that explode in the same way *E. deccanensis* seed pods did.

SPREADING SEEDS

The first land plants spread by spores. Today, seed plants far outnumber spore plants. This is partly because seeds can spread in many ways. Some seeds travel by wind and water. Others are spread by animals that eat fruit and nuts and then defecate their seeds. *E. deccanensis* is an example of a plant that had its own method of spreading seeds without outside help.

Pressure built inside the fruit's chambers until it exploded. This sent seeds and pieces flying out, helping the plant spread. Fibers present in the fruit fossils are similar to those of modern plants that spread seeds in a similar way.

HOT SPOT

Petrified fossils of *E. deccanensis* were found in India's Deccan Traps. Near the end of the Cretaceous Period, this landmass passed over a hot area of Earth's crust. The heat formed volcanoes that erupted for about 30,000 years. *E. deccanensis* and other organisms were quickly covered with ash. Then the land flooded. The water may have come from nearby volcanic hot springs loaded with minerals. These are ideal conditions for creating fossils. As a result, the Deccan Traps are a fossil-rich area.

Florissantia likely grew near lakes in volcanic areas.

FLORISSANTIA

Florissantia was a flowering plant that grew about 34 million years ago. Its fossils are uncommon. When they are found, they show a flower with five petals. Dark veins run from the center to the ends of the petals. These veins carried food and water.

Scientists have found fossilized *Florissantia* pollen in addition to flowers. Insects and birds spread this pollen. Wind may have also blown pollen to other plants. This allowed *Florissantia* to reproduce.

A SPECIAL SITE

The name *Florissantia* comes from the Florissant Fossil Beds in Colorado. Paleontologists discovered *Florissantia* fossils at this site. Flowers are not commonly fossilized because they are delicate. But the muddy conditions at Florissant preserved a full *Florissantia* flower.

DID YOU KNOW?

Flower fossils are rare. But wildfires preserved thousands of microscopic, blooming flowers in charcoal.

More than 1,800 species of fossils have been found at Florissant, including the wasp *Palaeovespa florissantia*. Wasps help spread pollen, allowing plants to reproduce.

GINKGO

Ginkgo is a genus of gymnosperm trees. A gymnosperm is a plant with seeds that are fully exposed. Fossilized *Ginkgo* leaves are distinctive and commonly found.

THROUGHOUT HISTORY

Scientists have used the abundant fossils of this genus to trace its range throughout geologic history. The oldest fossils date back about

Many *Ginkgo* leaf fossils have a fan shape that is identical to that of living *Ginkgo* trees' leaves.

Ginkgo biloba is known as a living fossil. No other living plant is closely related to this species.

290 million years. Rocks show that *Ginkgo* species spread throughout the world. However, *Ginkgo* fossils are uncommon in rocks that are younger than two million years old. The genus was scarce for a time. Eventually, in about 1000 CE, Buddhist monks cultivated *Ginkgo* trees, and the modern species, *Ginkgo biloba*, spread around the world once again.

Sculptures representing living *Lepidodendron* stand in the Evolution Garden of Singapore Botanic Gardens.

LEPIDODENDRON

Lepidodendron was a tree-sized club moss. It grew to be about 148 feet (45 m) tall. Club mosses are evergreen vascular plants that reproduce with spores. *Lepidodendron* means "scale tree." Fossilized *Lepidodendron* bark shows diamond-shaped patterns. These patterns resemble scales, but they were created by leaves that were once attached to the trunk. As the plant grew, the leaves broke off and left behind scars.

COAL SOURCE

Lepidodendron was a common plant in peat forests. These forests were hot and humid swamps in low-lying areas. Ancient club mosses thrived there about 360 to 300 million years ago. Much of the world's coal formed during this time. Dead plants piled up in the swamps and were covered by water and sediment. They turned into a decomposed matter called peat. Over millions of years, pressure and high temperatures petrified the buried peat and turned it into coal.

Paleontologists have found several *Lepidodendron* fossils in areas where coal is mined.

MAGNOLIA

Trees in the *Magnolia* genus were some of Earth's first flowering trees. They appeared more than 100 million years ago. *Magnolia* leaves are commonly found fossils. They share features with their modern relatives.

RECONSTRUCTING FLOWERS

No fossilized remains of *Magnolia* flowers have been identified. But this genus is a living fossil. More than 200 species of *Magnolia* exist throughout the world today. Scientists have used modern *Magnolia* trees to reconstruct missing parts of the ancient trees' biology.

Magnolia trees reproduced with pollen from their flowers. Since *Magnolia* trees existed before bees, they were first pollinated by beetles. The ancient flowers were thicker than modern flowers to survive damage from the beetles' jaws.

A *Magnolia* leaf fossil has a long, oval shape with a pointed end. It also has a large vein in the center with smaller veins branching off from it.

Scientists learn about ancient *Magnolia* species by studying their living relatives. Ancient *Magnolia* flowers likely had bowl-shaped petals, similar to those of modern *Magnolia* species.

Rhynia stem cross sections show clusters of circles called vessels. These vessels carried water, food, and minerals from the ground through the plant.

RHYNIA

Rhynia was a small, Paleozoic land plant. Its leafless stem branched in a V pattern. Each side ended with a spore sac. Scientists have studied cross sections of fossilized *Rhynia* stems under a microscope. They have observed that the stem has an outer skin and a small, dark center.

Rhynia was one of the earliest plants to grow on land. Its stem was strong enough to support its weight. It did not need to float in water to stay upright.

MINERAL WATER

Rhynia is named after the Scottish village of Rhynie, where its fossils were first discovered. The area around Rhynie was once a swamp with hot springs. Sometimes the hot springs flooded the land and drowned the plants. Then, mud and mineral-rich water covered everything. Over time, minerals seeped through the sediment and replaced the cells of organisms buried there. Many *Rhynia* fossils were petrified through this process.

Artists have imagined what *Rhynia* may have looked like in its habitat. Some elements of artistic renditions may be inaccurate, such as leafy stems.

SASSAFRAS

Ancient *Sassafras* was a flowering tree that lived about 100 million years ago. Ancient *Sassafras* trees could grow up to 100 feet (30 m) tall. They mainly populated woodlands with mild climates.

DID YOU KNOW?

Modern *Sassafras* trees are well known for their fragrant oil, bark, and roots. People use these parts of the plant to flavor drinks and foods. Root beer was first made with *Sassafras* roots.

The *Sassafras* genus has three living species, which makes it a living fossil.

COLORFUL FOSSILS

Most fossilized *Sassafras* leaves have three lobes. Scientists have found that some natural plant colors, including those in *Sassafras* leaves, can survive the fossilization process. This is because some plants have porphyrins. These are a type of pigment, or substance that provides color, that resists decay.

Petrified *Sassafras* leaves can be reddish gold and brown.

A cut stromatolite reveals layers of fossilized algae.

STROMATOLITES

Stromatolites are made of layers of cyanobacteria, which are a type of blue-green algae. The algae form sticky mats. These mats trap sand and soil. Then more algae grow over the sediment. The layering process continues for many years.

DID YOU KNOW?

NASA sent a rover to Mars in 2020 to collect Martian rocks and soil. Scientists are looking for signs of ancient microbial life. They are looking for stromatolites and similar fossils.

It may take 2,000 to 3,000 years to create a stromatolite that is 3 feet (1 m) tall. Only the top layer of a stromatolite is alive. The algae beneath it are smothered and die.

OLDEST LIVING FOSSIL

Stromatolites existed more than three billion years ago, and they still grow today. This makes them the planet's oldest living fossils. But they can survive only in very salty water. They grow in only a handful of places today. Most live in the shallow waters of lagoons and bays.

Many stromatolites resemble round boulders. Australia, Mexico, and the Bahamas are some of the countries where they can be found.

AMMONITES

Ammonites were ancestors of the modern nautilus. They lived all over the world. Ammonites were part of the mollusk group of marine cephalopods. Mollusks are soft-bodied invertebrates, and cephalopods are those that have large heads and tentacles.

Early cephalopods, including ammonites, grew hard shells to protect themselves. The outer shells often had evenly spaced segments that spiraled inward. Ammonite shells have been mistaken for coiled snakes and rams' horns.

ABUNDANT FOSSILS

Experts have identified more than 10,000 species of ammonites from fossilized remains. These diverse cephalopods lived around the world from 416 to 66 million years ago. They ranged in size from 1 inch (2.5 cm) to 9 feet (2.7 m) across.

The interior of an ammonite fossil displays many chambers separated by thin walls. The animal lived in the outer chamber. The others were filled with gases or fluids.

Ammonites are among the most commonly found fossils.

Three-dimensional models created from CT scans show much more detail than fossils alone. This model comes from a 100-million-year-old cockroach.

ARCHIMYLACRIS EGGINTONI

Archimylacris eggintoni was an insect. It was an ancestor of the modern cockroach. Insect fossils are extremely rare because these organisms lack bones and teeth. When fossilized, insects can be difficult to remove from surrounding rock. Many insect fossils, especially those of the limbs, are small and fragile.

Archimylacris eggintoni is more than 350 million years old.

SCANNING FOSSILS

In 2010, despite its fragile fossils, scientists re-created *A. eggintoni*. They did this by using a CT scanner on a fossil containing *A. eggintoni* body parts. A CT scanner takes two-dimensional X-ray pictures that can be used to create a three-dimensional image.

For *A. eggintoni*, the machine took 3,142 X-ray images. Scientists used a computer program to produce a three-dimensional model of what the insect probably looked like. The model revealed that *A. eggintoni* had legs that were quick and moved easily.

A park in Germany displayed a model of what *Arthropleura* may have looked like when alive.

ARTHROPLEURA

Arthropleura was an arthropod related to millipedes. An arthropod is an invertebrate with jointed limbs, body segments, and a shell covering its body called an exoskeleton. In 2018, a paleontology student found a partial *Arthropleura* fossil while hiking on a cliff in England. At 30 inches (76 cm) long and 14 inches (36 cm) wide, it is the largest *Arthropleura* fossil ever found. Experts believe that the fossil formed when the arthropod shed its exoskeleton next to a river. Sediment covered the exoskeleton and petrified it.

GIANT MILLIPEDE

Arthropleura was one of the largest invertebrates to ever live. The full size of the partially fossilized *Arthropleura* found in 2018 would have been about 8.5 feet (2.6 m) long and 1.8 feet (0.5 m) wide. It weighed about 110 pounds (50 kg). *Arthropleura* lived in open, woody places during the Paleozoic Era. *Arthropleura* was a detritivore. This means it fed on dead or decaying plant and animal matter.

Arthropleura had many pairs of short legs. Some fossils show parts of the organism's legs.

BELEMNITELLA

Belemnitella was a squid-like cephalopod. Its name comes from the Greek word for "dart" or "javelin." This is a reference to the shape of the animal's rostrum. The rostrum was at the rear of *Belemnitella*'s body. It was made from a hard material, so it was often the only part preserved as a fossil.

SQUID RELATIVES

Belemnitella belonged to an extinct group of cephalopods called belemnites. A few petrified fossils of belemnites have been found almost fully intact. This is how scientists know that belemnites looked similar to modern squid.

Belemnitella fossils show that the animal's rostrum grew over time. Cross sections show rings similar to those of trees.

A modern squid does not have a hard skeleton or rostrum, but *Belemnitella* did.

DID YOU KNOW?

Belemnites had ink sacs similar to those of octopuses. A researcher mixed fossilized belemnite ink with ammonia to make the ink soft. Then he used the ink to draw a picture of a belemnite.

A *Cantabrigiaster fezouataensis* fossil shows wavy orange-and-brown threads called ossicles. Ossicles are thin, bone-like structures.

CANTABRIGIASTER FEZOUATAENSIS

Cantabrigiaster fezouataensis is an ancient relative of modern sea stars. In Morocco, scientists discovered a *C. fezouataensis* fossil from an organism that lived about 480 million years ago. This is the oldest sea star–like species yet discovered. The organism lived in a cold-water reef near what is now Antarctica. As continents shifted, the rock containing its fossil moved. Parts of the petrified fossil are missing. But at least some of each of the five limbs remain. The five points extend out from its mouth in the center.

STUDYING SEA STARS

Scientists have studied other sea star fossils to learn more about *C. fezouataensis*. This organism may have crawled along the seafloor with tube-like feet. It was likely a predator. But fossils do not reveal what it ate.

C. fezouataensis was likely a relative of brittle stars. Brittle stars have long, thin arms.

CHACEON PERUVIANUS

Chaceon peruvianus was a crab that lived in shallow marine waters during the Cenozoic Era. Most of the time, the claws are the only part of a crab that fossilizes. The claws are the hardest part of crab bodies. But some fossilized crabs such as *C. peruvianus* have been found fully intact. This is because they are surrounded by a hard mass called a concretion.

CONCRETIONS

A concretion was created when the dead crab was buried quickly. As it decayed, the

An intact fossil of *Chaceon peruvianus* shows that, like modern crabs, it was a decapod. A decapod is a crustacean with five pairs of legs. The front pair had pincers.

crab released minerals called phosphates. The phosphates turned the minerals around the body into cement. These minerals also hardened the body.

Concretions often resemble smooth rocks. Or they may take the shape of the fossil preserved inside them. They are usually embedded in sedimentary rock. They may be cracked open to reveal the fossil inside. Scientists once thought it took millions of years for concretions to form. But new research suggests it may take only a few months or years for cementing minerals to develop and harden.

EURYPTERUS

Eurypterus was a marine arthropod that resembled a giant sea scorpion. Many *Eurypterus* fossils are exoskeletons that the arthropod shed and then regrew throughout its life. It had jointed, paddle-like limbs used for swimming. Above the paddles were four pairs of legs. *Eurypterus* used these to walk on the ocean floor. The arthropod also had a pair of pincers to draw food into its mouth.

A *Eurypterus* fossil shows a segmented body that narrows to a scorpion-like tail.

Trace fossils show tracks where *Eurypterus* moved along the ground as it exited the water.

LARGEST FOSSIL

Eurypterus swam in coastal waters between 430 and 410 million years ago. The largest *Eurypterus* fossil ever found is on display at the Paleontological Research Institution in Ithaca, New York. It is more than 4 feet (1.2 m) long. *Eurypterus* was about 8 inches (20 cm) long on average. *Eurypterus* is the official state fossil of New York because these fossils are so abundant there.

Scientists first thought the round shape at the end of a *Hallucigenia* fossil was its head. They later learned this was matter from the creature's rear end that came out as the organism decayed.

HALLUCIGENIA

Hallucigenia had a bizarre appearance. This led to its name, which means "imaginary." The worm-like creature lived 510 million years ago. The first *Hallucigenia* fossil was described in 1911. Researchers initially thought this marine animal had long, floppy legs. Others believed it had tentacles with mouths extending from its back for grasping food. Its head appeared large and bulbous. But later *Hallucigenia* fossils were often missing a head.

The anatomy of *Hallucigenia* was revised in the 1990s when some complete fossils were discovered. Scientists learned that they had the creature all wrong. What they thought were legs were actually defensive spikes on its back. Its mouths were actually feet with claws. Scientists also had the creature backward. What they thought was its rear end was its head.

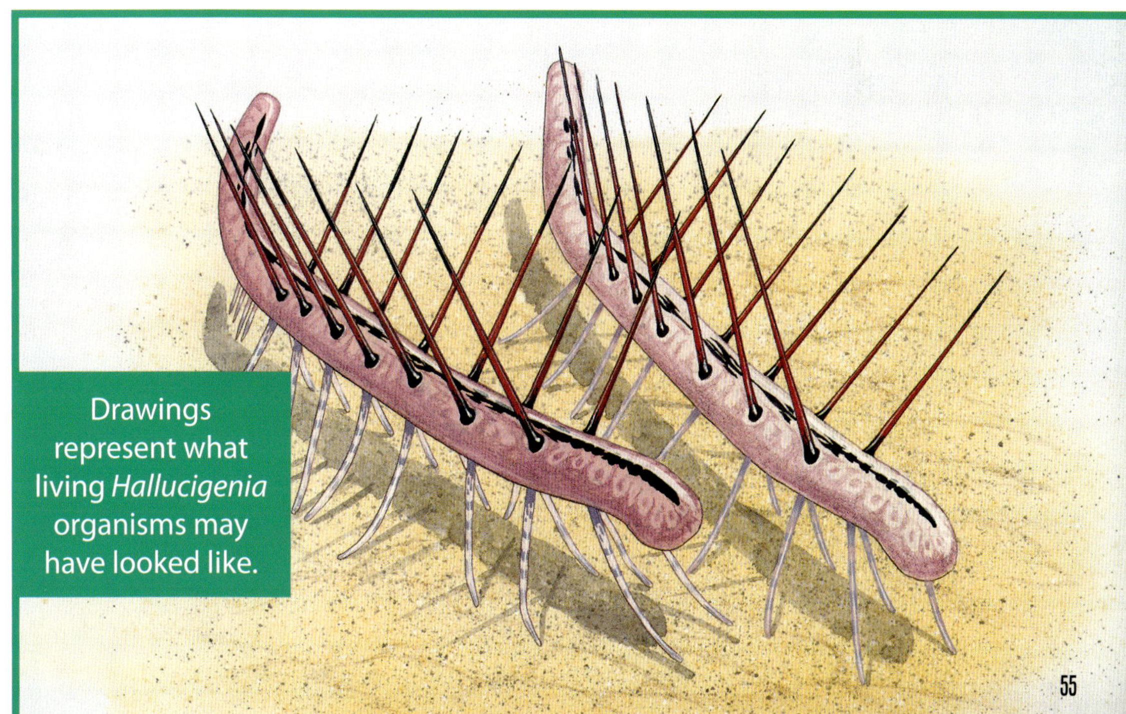

Drawings represent what living *Hallucigenia* organisms may have looked like.

Researchers have discovered some nearly complete *Meganeura* fossils.

MEGANEURA

Meganeura was a giant insect that resembled a dragonfly. Most fossils of this insect are fragmented and poorly preserved. *Meganeura* had four wings attached to a long, segmented body. Experts think *Meganeura*'s wingspan was 28 inches (71 cm). This is close to the wingspan of a pigeon.

GIANT INSECTS

Meganeura fossils are rare. Paleontologists found the first fossils in 1880 in a French coal deposit. About 100 years later, workers found another *Meganeura* fossil in a British coal mine.

Fossils trapped in coal tell paleontologists that the organism lived during the Carboniferous Period, about 300 million years ago. The atmosphere during this period was 35 percent oxygen. Today it is about 21 percent oxygen. An oxygen-rich environment likely led to the giant size of insects such as *Meganeura*.

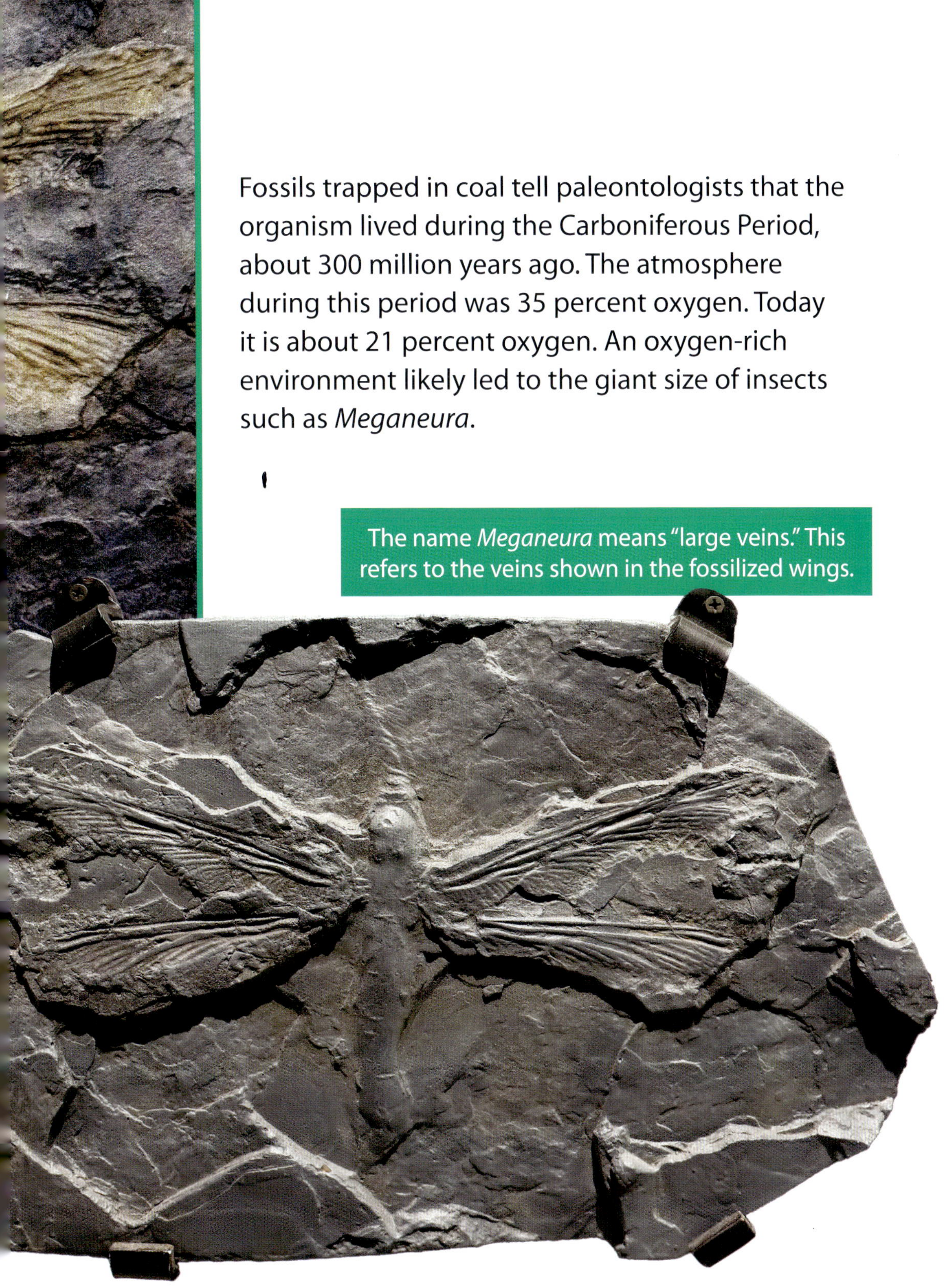

The name *Meganeura* means "large veins." This refers to the veins shown in the fossilized wings.

MESOLIMULUS

Mesolimulus was a horseshoe crab that lived in shallow coastal waters during the Mesozoic Era. *Mesolimulus* fossils are common. Some of the best-preserved fossils were discovered in Germany's Solnhofen Limestone.

A complete fossil shows that *Mesolimulus* had a large, semicircular shield similar to those of other horseshoe crabs. This shield covers its head. Below the shield was a spiky abdomen. It had a long, slender tail. *Mesolimulus* was about 5 inches (13 cm) long on average.

LIVING FOSSILS

Mesolimulus was named after the modern horseshoe crab, *Limulus polyphemus*. They are almost identical. This makes *L. polyphemus* a living fossil. Studying *L. polyphemus* tells researchers about how *Mesolimulus* may have lived.

SOLNHOFEN LIMESTONE

Solnhofen Limestone comes from an area that was once filled with marine lagoons. These were too salty and toxic to sustain most life, especially at the bottom. There were no scavengers to eat dead organisms that fell or were washed in. Lagoon muds gradually covered dead organisms. These sediments preserved many fully intact organisms, including *Mesolimulus*.

Mesolimulus is distantly related to spiders and scorpions.

MONGOLARACHNE JURASSICA

The classification of fossils can change as more fossils are uncovered. In 2005, the largest known spider fossil was found in China. The body of the female spider was about 1 inch (2.5 cm) long. At the time, scientists identified the fossil as a Jurassic ancestor of the golden orb-weaver spider, in the family Nephilidae. They named the extinct species *Nephila jurassica*.

However, a few years later, a male spider was found near where the female was found. Both fossils were similar in age

The male *Mongolarachne jurassica* spider, *left*, had slightly longer legs than the female spider, *right*.

M. jurassica was likely related to modern spiders in the Deinopidae family. These are known as net casting spiders.

and size. The female's body was slightly longer and thicker. The fossilized male spider did not resemble Nephilidae males. Researchers decided that both fossilized spiders belonged to a new species called *Mongolarachne jurassica*.

RARE FOSSILS

Spider fossils are extremely rare. Like many insects, spiders are delicate. They are easy to squish. They do not have a skeleton or shell to protect them when they die. Most also avoid bodies of water. Sometimes spiders are fossilized in amber. But the *M. jurassica* spiders likely lived near a volcano that exploded. The blast may have swept them to the bottom of a nearby lake. Then sediment covered them, and the fossilization process began.

Nummulites could live for up to 100 years.

NUMMULITES

Nummulites were single-celled organisms that lived in warm, shallow marine waters. Many inhabited the Tethys Ocean during the Cenozoic Era. The area is now the Middle East and North Africa.

The name *nummulites* means "little coins" in Latin. This is a reference to their disc shape. Their fossils can reach up to 6 inches (15 cm) in diameter. They often show imprints of the organism's coiled shape. Scientists think algae called diatoms helped these animals grow their skeletons.

BUILDING BLOCKS

Billions of nummulites once covered the ocean floor. After they died, the remains were quickly covered with sand. As they decomposed and were compressed by the sand and water, the mixture of remains and sand turned into a rock called nummulite limestone. It was one of the materials used to build the Pyramids of Giza in Egypt. The ancient Greek historian Herodotus was the first to write about nummulites. He noticed them in the stones of the pyramids.

Nummulite limestone can be found in the Sahara desert.

PENTREMITES

Pentremites was a blastoid that lived 359 to 299 million years ago. A blastoid is an extinct type of marine echinoderm. Echinoderms are invertebrates that have bumps or spines on their bodies. The head, called a theca, of *Pentremites* was small and commonly fossilized. Many of these fossils are less than 0.5 inches (1.3 cm) in diameter.

Pentremites had bristle-like structures on it that fossilized separately from the blastoid or were not preserved.

The bottom of a *Pentremites* fossil shows a bump where the head connected to the stem.

A *Pentremites* fossil looks like a nut with a flower wrapped around it. The fossil shows a hole on the top of the head, which was its mouth. The structures that resemble petals are called ambulacra. The ambulacra helped gather food and direct it toward the mouth. The mouth was surrounded by holes it used to breathe and one it used to release digested food. A stem grew from the bottom that connected the head to the seafloor. But fossils of *Pentremites* heads are rarely attached to the stems.

INDEX FOSSILS

Only a few fossils have been found of many kinds of ancient echinoderms. But *Pentremites* are so abundant that scientists use them as an index fossil. This means scientists can determine the age of a rock if they find *Pentremites* fossils in it.

RUDISTS

Rudists were Cretaceous bivalve mollusks related to clams. Bivalves are aquatic animals that live inside two hard shells connected by a hinge. There were many species of rudists. Their shapes varied widely. Paleontologists have discovered straight, coiled, and curved rudists. Some rudists were thin and flat, while others were thick and cylindrical. One could resemble a ram's horn, a snail, or a cup. A rudist fossil of *Hippurites radiosus*

Caprina adversa was a rudist with a coiled shape. It lived about 100 million years ago.

looks like a curved cone with a lid. While living, the top was hinged so it could open and close.

OIL FIELDS

Rudists lived in the shallow waters of tropical seas. Rudists were the only mollusks to form huge reefs. Reefs are natural structures in the ocean. Today, many reefs are made of corals. But long ago, rudist reefs stretched hundreds of miles long and hundreds of feet tall. After rudists died, their reefs turned into giant piles of shells. These shells fossilized and formed barriers that trapped decaying matter beneath them. Some of this matter became oil deposits that are drilled today.

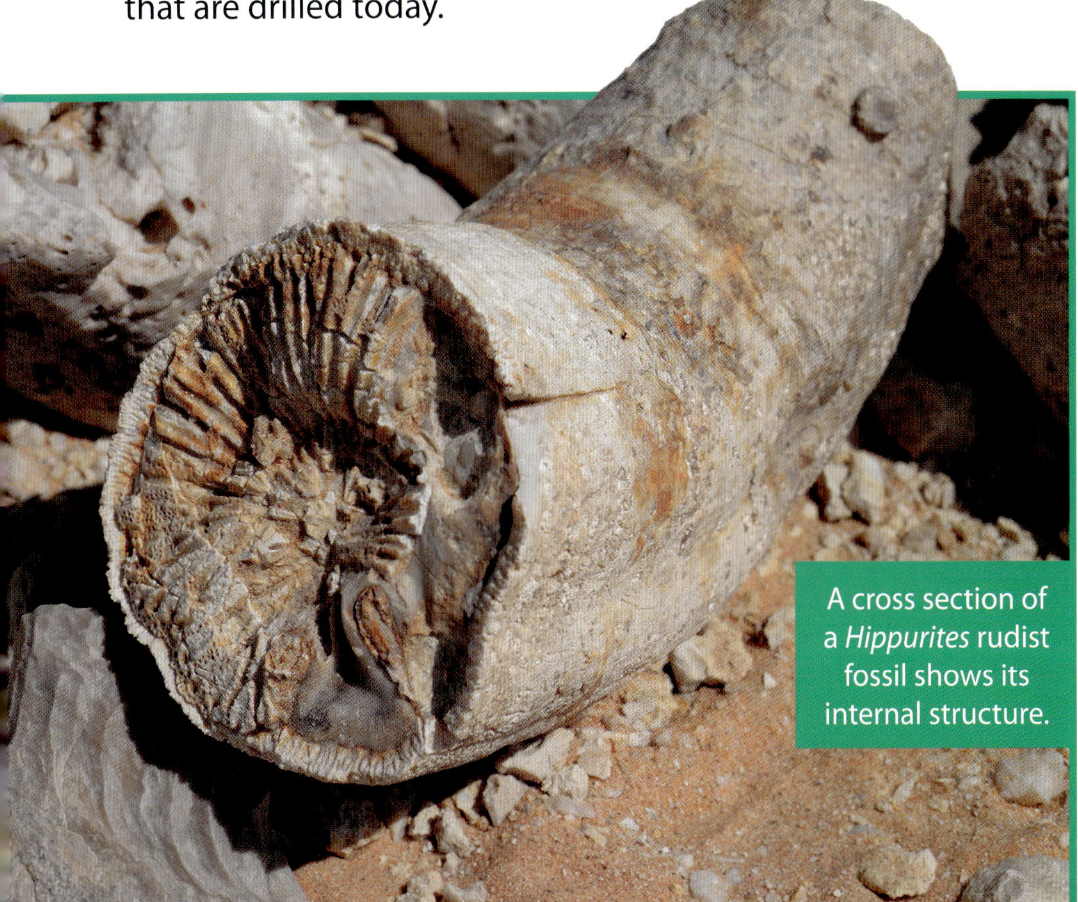

A cross section of a *Hippurites* rudist fossil shows its internal structure.

SPONGES

Sponges are animals that live on ocean floors. They have changed little over time. Modern sponges are considered living fossils. Sponges are simple organisms. A sponge does not have a brain, stomach, or nervous system. As water moves through the sponge, it brings food and oxygen to the organism and flushes out waste. Many ancient sponges were soft, making fossils of these species rare. Some species of sponges had hard structures called spicules that formed a supportive skeleton. These are the body parts that most often fossilized.

SPONGE VARIETY

Sponges have lived in the ocean for longer than any other type of animal. A discovery in Canada in the early 2000s dates

Today there are about 5,000 species of living sponges.

sponges back about 890 million years. They may form in shapes similar to tubes, plates, flowers, or mushrooms. Some fossilized sponges resemble rocks with microscopic lines showing the animals' texture. Others reveal net-like structures of spicules.

Sponge fossils are not commonly found.

TRILOBITES

Trilobite means "three lobes" in Greek. These marine arthropods lived during the Paleozoic Era. They thrived around the world for 270 million years. Thanks to their hard exoskeletons, many trilobites survived fossilization intact.

A fossil from the genus *Calymene* shows typical trilobite anatomy. The body has a central lobe with one lobe on each side. The lobes are segmented. The fossil also has a semicircular

Fossils of more than 20,000 species of trilobites have been discovered so far.

A detailed *Erbenochile* fossil shows that this genus had hundreds of lenses in its eyes.

head shield. Like most trilobites, *Calymene* was small. It was about 2 inches (5 cm) long on average.

EARLY EYES

Trilobites may have been the first animals with complex eyes. The genus *Erbenochile* had eyes shaped like two towers. This gave it 360-degree vision. One *Erbenochile* fossil dates back 400 million years. It is ancient, but its eyes are well preserved. This is because they were made from calcite. This hard mineral fossilized well.

TYLOCIDARIS

Tylocidaris was a sea urchin that lived on the ocean floor during the Mesozoic Era. Many *Tylocidaris* fossils have been found in Europe and North America. They show a rounded body with rings all over where the spines were once attached. Most modern sea urchins have thin, sharp spines. But the spines of *Tylocidaris* fossils resemble clubs. They are thick and have rows of thorns that run along their sides. These spines likely kept predators away.

BREAKING UP

It is common to find the fossilized parts of sea urchins. Their bodies and spines are made of calcite, which preserves well. Many *Tylocidaris* fossils have been discovered in British chalk. But it is much less common to find an intact fossil. After death, spines usually broke away from the body before fossilization could begin.

A detailed fossil from London's Natural History Museum shows *Tylocidaris* and its club-like spines.

Modern sea urchins have needle-like spines. Some contain poison.

AQUATIC VERTEBRATES AND AMPHIBIANS

ARCHELON

Archelon was a giant sea turtle that lived between 75 and 66 million years ago. A life-size replica of *Archelon* is suspended from the ceiling of the Yale Peabody Museum in New Haven, Connecticut. The replica is based on an *Archelon* fossil found in the 1890s. This fossil is about 13 feet (4 m) long and 16 feet (4.8 m) wide. However, it is too fragile to be hung in the air. So scientists scanned its bones and created a replica.

An *Archelon ischyodus* skeleton is part of the collection at the Royal Ontario Museum in Toronto, Canada.

Artists have created images of what *Archelon* may have looked like based on its fossils.

BUILT TO SWIM

Based on fossils and comparisons to other turtles, scientists think *Archelon*'s shell was leathery instead of hard. This made the shell lighter so it was easier for *Archelon* to swim. The Peabody *Archelon* has two pairs of giant flippers. It also shows the turtle's powerful beak. *Archelon* likely crushed and ate marine animals such as jellyfish and crustaceans. Although *Archelon* was large, it was prey for other animals. It could not draw in its head or flippers.

A *Basilosaurus* skull shows that its blowhole, where it breathed, was located in front of its eyes. The blowholes of most modern whales are located between or behind the eyes.

BASILOSAURUS

Basilosaurus was a whale that lived in oceans around the world during the Cenozoic Era. A complete skeleton hangs in the National Museum of Natural History in Washington, DC. It is about 52 feet (16 m) long. It shows that *Basilosaurus* resembled a giant eel. It had four small limbs. But the back limbs, which had knees and toes, were too small to help the whale swim. The skull had back teeth that were triangular and serrated. These teeth are evidence that *Basilosaurus* was likely a mammal.

DID YOU KNOW?

Basilosaurus means "king lizard." When this genus was first discovered, scientists thought it was a reptile and named it like a dinosaur. They later learned it was a mammal.

FINDING *BASILOSAURUS*

It took researchers more than 150 years to put together a complete *Basilosaurus* skeleton. A single *Basilosaurus* vertebra and additional fragments were described in 1834. Over the years, more bone fragments were added to the puzzle. Finally, in 2005, a complete skeleton was discovered in a desert in Egypt. A second expedition yielded another complete fossil with its stomach contents intact. This is how scientists learned *Basilosaurus* ate bony fish, sharks, sea cows, and even other whales.

Several *Basilosaurus* vertebrae were found in Egypt at Wadi Al-Hitan. This paleontological site is now protected, and some fossils remain on display there.

DEINOSUCHUS

Deinosuchus was a predator that lived 82 to 75 million years ago. Its name means "terror crocodile." A reconstructed *Deinosuchus* skeleton is on display at the Natural History Museum of Utah. It shows a four-legged reptile with limbs coming off the sides of its body rather than from underneath. The skull has a long snout that is filled with sharp, conical teeth. The eye sockets are on top of its head.

A replica of a *Deinosuchus* skull is displayed in Big Bend National Park in Texas.

Deinosuchus likely preyed on dinosaurs.

FIERCE PREDATOR

Based on fossils, scientists believe that *Deinosuchus* grew to the size of a school bus. It was more than 30 feet (9 m) long and weighed about 8,000 pounds (3,600 kg). A study of its jaw suggests it had a strong bite force that may have rivaled that of *Tyrannosaurus rex*.

Deinosuchus did not chew its food. Researchers have learned from its fossilized poop, called coprolites, that it swallowed its prey whole. Coprolites can tell researchers a lot about the eating habits of extinct species.

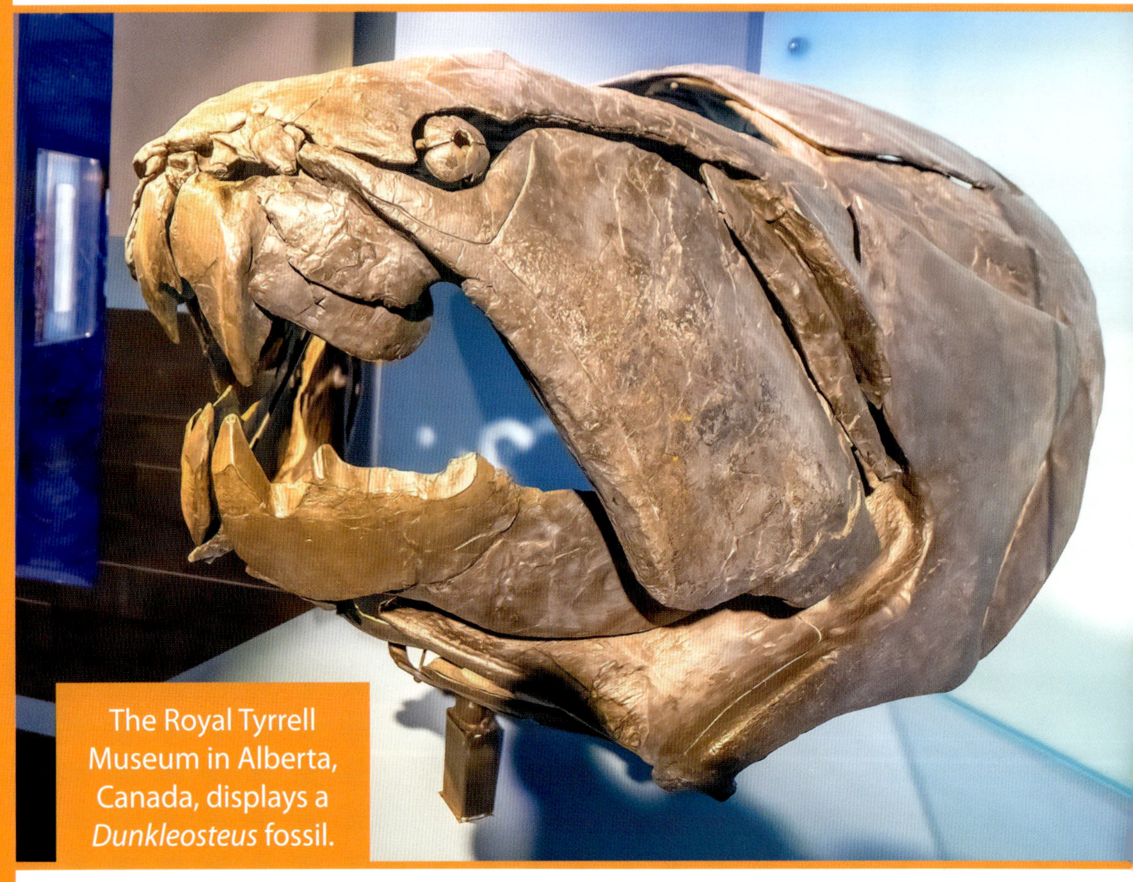

The Royal Tyrrell Museum in Alberta, Canada, displays a *Dunkleosteus* fossil.

DUNKLEOSTEUS

Dunkleosteus was an armored fish that lived between 419 and 360 million years ago. At that time, it may have been the world's largest predator. A cast of a *Dunkleosteus* fossil is on display at the Cleveland Museum of Natural History. It shows a head covered with hard plates of armor. The fish's jaws have no teeth. Instead, there are sharpened, exposed bones. When *Dunkleosteus* opened and closed its mouth, these bones acted like scissors and sliced through prey.

ESTIMATING SIZE

Most *Dunkleosteus* fossils consist of only the bony plates that covered its head and trunk. The rest of the predator's body was likely made from cartilage that was too soft to become fossilized. So scientists have studied other fish, both living and extinct, to reconstruct *Dunkleosteus*. For example, they assumed that most predatory fish have similar proportions. Based on that, they estimated that *Dunkleosteus* grew to be about 30 feet (9 m) long and weighed about 8,800 pounds (4,000 kg).

The head and trunk plates of *Dunkleosteus* were made from strong minerals that fossilized well.

ELECTRORANA LIMOAE

Electrorana limoae was a small frog that lived in wet, tropical forests about 99 million years ago. The only fossil of this ancient frog was found in Myanmar. It is preserved in amber. The frog is less than 1 inch (2.5 cm) long. Its skull, its front legs, part of the backbone, and part of a back leg are visible in the fossil. But certain bones are missing. These include the wristbones and hip bones. The frog was likely still growing. Its skeleton had not fully developed.

TROPICAL NEIGHBORS

Many modern frogs live in tropical forests around the world. But *E. limoae* is the first fossil to show that ancient frogs also lived in these environments. To understand the ancient frog's habitat, scientists compared this fossil to other amber fossils from the same area. The other fossils included bamboo-like plants that grow only in the tropics. This revealed the tropical habitat of *E. limoae*.

AMBER

Few frog fossils have been found. Most frogs were probably too delicate. *E. limoae* is one of the oldest frog fossils preserved in amber. Amber itself is a fossil. It forms a protective coat against oxygen and other factors that cause decay. It helps embalm the organism.

Electrorana limoae was preserved alongside a beetle and other organic matter.

ERYOPS

Eryops was a prehistoric amphibian that resembled a crocodile. It lived during the Paleozoic Era. A complete *Eryops* skeleton is part of the fossil collection at the American Museum of Natural History in New York City. It shows a long skull with eye sockets pointing upward. The bones of its limbs are thick and sturdy. It has a long tail.

A museum staff member works on an *Eryops* skeleton belonging to the Field Museum in Chicago, Illinois.

Researchers have found an abundance of *Eryops* skeletons.

Eryops was about 6 feet (1.8 m) long on average. It weighed between 220 and 485 pounds (100 and 220 kg). Its sharp teeth could pierce prey such as fish and small land animals. But its jaw was not designed for chewing. *Eryops* swallowed most of its prey whole.

DESERT DISCOVERIES

Many *Eryops* skeletons have been found in the desert rocks of Texas and New Mexico. These areas once held swamps, ponds, and rivers. *Eryops* may have been an early animal species that evolved to walk on land instead of only swimming in water.

Some scientists believed the tooth whorl had been part of a tail.

HELICOPRION

The name *Helicoprion* means "spiral saw." This refers to the tooth whorl in this shark-like fish. *Helicoprion* swam in oceans around the world between 290 and 250 million years ago. But only its teeth have survived as fossils in most cases.

A fossilized whorl shows that small, triangular teeth grew larger as they spiraled away from the center of the jaw. The smaller teeth were newer and pushed older, larger ones away as they grew in. *Helicoprion* teeth had different roles depending on where they were placed. The front teeth hooked prey. The middle teeth pierced and cut it. The back teeth pushed food into the throat.

TOOTHY DEBATE

Experts began to debate the placement of *Helicoprion*'s tooth whorl as early as 1899. Some believed it had teeth on its nose or on other parts of its body. Others argued the fossils were not teeth but spines. Then, in 2013, scientists used a CT scanner to produce three-dimensional images of a whorl buried in a rock slab. Based on these images, scientists concluded that the whorl fit into *Helicoprion*'s lower jaw.

Artist renditions show how the tooth whorl made up the entire lower jaw of *Helicoprion.*

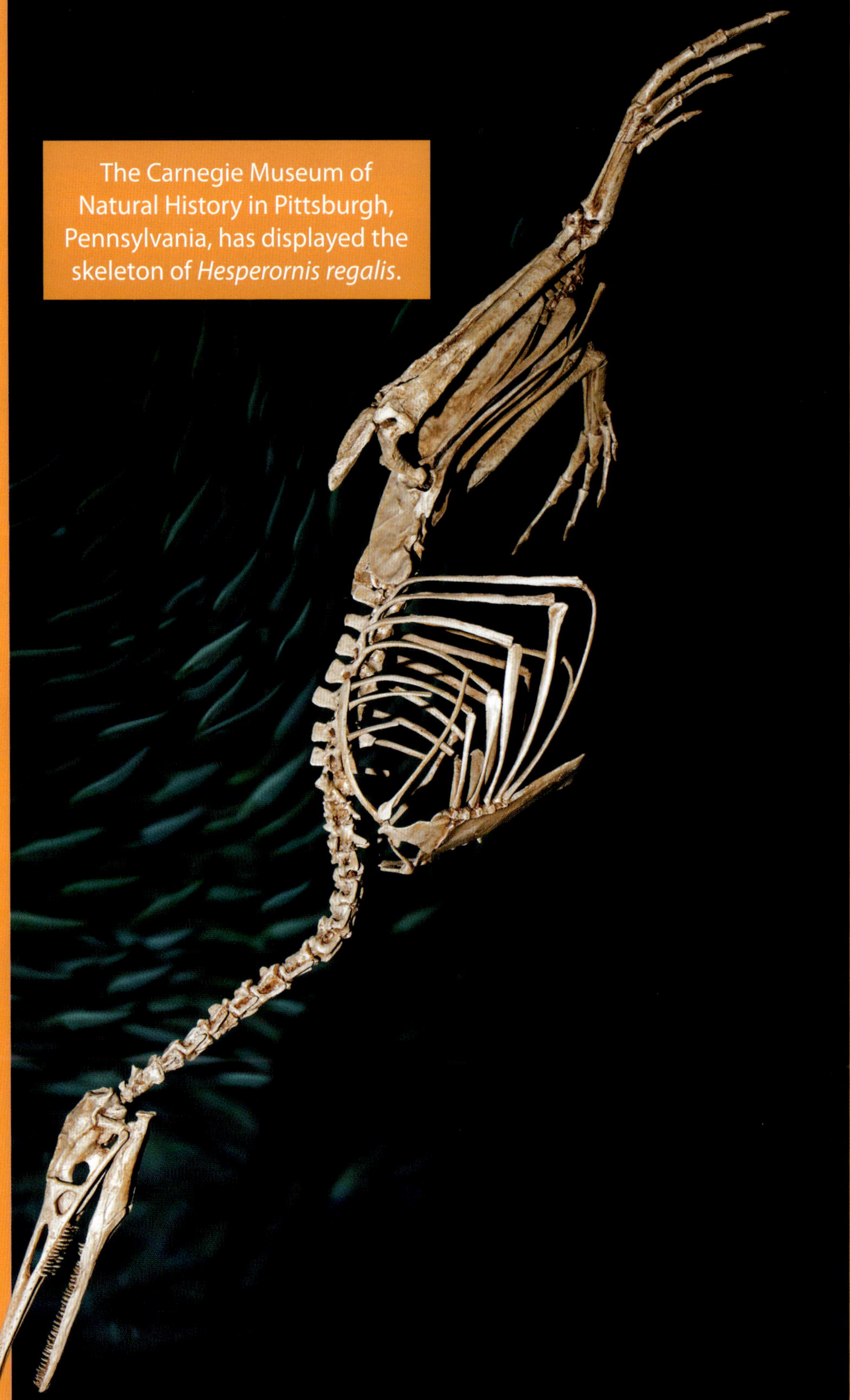

The Carnegie Museum of Natural History in Pittsburgh, Pennsylvania, has displayed the skeleton of *Hesperornis regalis*.

HESPERORNIS

Hesperornis was a genus of flightless seabird that lived 100 to 66 million years ago. A skeleton is part of the collection at the Yale Peabody Museum. It shows a thick body with a long, slender neck and skull. At the back of the body are long legs with large feet. *Hesperornis* had tiny wings.

This body structure suggests the bird could not fly but was a good swimmer. Its large legs paddled its body through the water. Its wings helped to steer.

EAR FOSSILS

Scientists research the inner ear fossils of *Hesperornis* and other animals related to modern birds. The shape of the inner ear can show whether an animal flew, walked, or swam. Researchers used a CT scanner to make a model of *Hesperornis*'s inner ear. They compared it to models of many animals' inner ears, both living and extinct, to confirm that this genus of bird swam.

Like modern loons, *Hesperornis* dived for its food.

ICHTHYOSAURUS

Ichthyosaur means "fish lizard." *Ichthyosaurus* is a genus of reptiles that lived during the Mesozoic Era. Their bodies had features similar to those of both fish and dolphins.

Ichthyosaurus had a thick body with a long skull and tail. Its long, dolphin-like beak was lined with sharp teeth. The eye sockets were large. These features suggest *Ichthyosaurus* hunted at night. *Ichthyosaurus* lived in water. Animals in this genus breathed air, meaning they came to the surface regularly. A complete skeleton of *Ichthyosaurus communis*

Some species of *Ichthyosaurus* were likely built similarly to modern tuna fish. This structure suggests *Ichthyosaurus* was a fast swimmer.

The presentation of this *Ichthyosaurus* fossil shows its dorsal fin. The soft tissue of this fin did not fossilize.

was found in England. This small *I. communis* fossil is about 28 inches (70 cm) long. But some species of *Ichthyosaurus* grew up to 60 feet (18 m) long.

YOUNG FOSSIL HUNTER

Ichthyosaurus fossils have been found all over the world. Mary Anning found one of the first fossils in 1811. She was 12 years old. Her complete fossil even had its last meal in its stomach. *Ichthyosaurus anningae* is named after her. Anning went on to become a paleontologist.

A cast fossil shows part of an *Ichthyostega* skull.

ICHTHYOSTEGA

Ichthyostega lived during the Paleozoic Era. The first fossils from this genus were discovered in Greenland in the 1930s. Many of the *Ichthyostega* fossils remained embedded in rock. The fossils could get damaged if they were removed. Details of the skeleton could be lost when it was cleaned. So in the 2000s, scientists used a CT scanner to create a replica of this animal.

TRANSITIONAL FOSSIL

Based on models and comparisons to other tetrapods, *Ichthyostega* likely could not walk. Instead, it used its four limbs to steer as it swam through the water. Scientists consider *Ichthyostega* to be a transitional fossil. This means it helps show how tetrapods shifted from living in water to living on land.

TETRAPODS THAT NEVER WALKED

Ichthyostega was a tetrapod. Tetrapod means "four feet." But not all tetrapods fit this description. A snake is a tetrapod. So are birds. This is because tetrapods are any animals that have an ancestor with four limbs. Some tetrapods, such as *Ichthyostega*, cannot walk even if they have four limbs.

On land, *Ichthyostega* may have moved like a mudskipper by flopping up and down.

LEPIDOTES

Lepidotes was a genus of both freshwater and marine fish that thrived during the Mesozoic Era. There is an abundance of *Lepidotes* fossils. Some show the exterior of an entire fish. Many fossils are of *Lepidotes* scales. Some scales are still shiny as fossils.

Researchers have identified more than 100 species of *Lepidotes* from around the world. There are so many species

Lepidotes scales are thick and diamond shaped. They are arranged in rows.

Lepidotes filled rivers, lakes, and coastal areas.

that scientists wonder whether some of the fossils classified as separate species are actually the same species. With such diversity, the estimated size of *Lepidotes* ranges from 12 inches (30 cm) to more than 6 feet (1.8 m) long.

TOADSTONES

Lepidotes had pebble-like teeth. People once thought its fossilized teeth were toadstones. Toadstones are mythical stones said to be found in a toad's head. They were thought to sweat, change color, or burn the skin when poison was present. So people wore jewelry made with *Lepidotes* fossils to protect themselves. People also swallowed them in an effort to cure various illnesses.

Many vertebrae bones have been found from *Mosasaurus* spines.

MOSASAURUS

Mosasaurus was a giant marine reptile. The Canadian Fossil Discovery Centre has the largest *Mosasaurus* skeleton. Its nickname is Bruce. The skeleton is 42 feet (13 m) long. It has about 70 percent of its original bones.

Several *Mosasaurus* skulls have been excavated. The jaw was double hinged. This feature is found in snake jaws. It allowed *Mosasaurus* to open its mouth extremely wide when attacking prey. *Mosasaurus* was an apex predator in the oceans between 145 and 65 million years ago. That means it was not prey to any other animal.

SPOILS OF WAR

Mosasaurus fossils have been found all over the world. But the first skull fragments were discovered in the Netherlands in 1764. Workers found them while digging in a limestone quarry. French general Napoleon Bonaparte learned about the fossil. He ordered his soldiers to bring it back to Paris. The skull has been on display at a Paris museum since 1795.

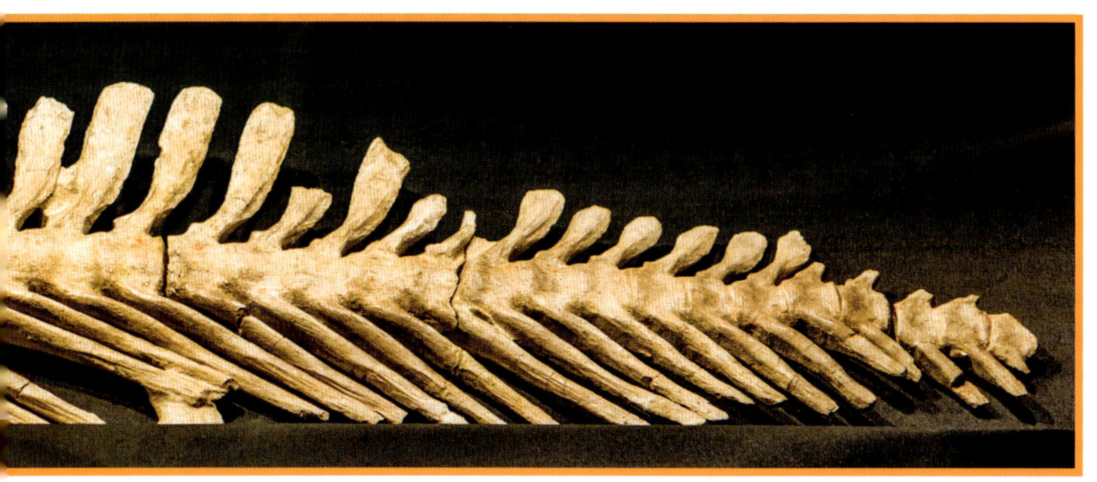

DID YOU KNOW?

Mosasaurus makes several appearances in the *Jurassic World* film franchise. This increased its popularity. Toymaker Mattel even made a *Mosasaurus* figure with movable parts.

Mosasaurus skulls show a second row of sharp, cone-shaped teeth on the roof of the mouth.

OTODUS MEGALODON

Otodus megalodon, commonly called megalodon, was a giant shark. It may have been the biggest shark to ever live. Megalodon fossils from the Cenozoic Era have been found on every continent except Antarctica. Almost all of these are fossilized teeth.

Megalodon's scientific name comes from Greek words meaning "giant tooth." Megalodon's triangular, serrated teeth could grow to the size of a human hand. In 2022, researchers

Megalodon could likely open its jaw to be about 6 feet (1.8 m) wide.

A megalodon tooth, *left*, can reach about 7 inches (18 cm) long. The tooth of a great white shark, *right*, is about 2 inches (5 cm) long.

found 53 megalodon teeth at the same location in Maryland. These teeth are likely from a single shark because they were found so close together.

SHARK TEETH

Shark teeth are common fossils. This is because they are made from a hard material called dentin. When a tooth fell out, it dropped to the ocean floor. Scavengers did not try to eat it. Sand, water, and time turned it into a fossil. A modern shark may lose more than 20,000 teeth in its lifetime. This might have been true of ancient sharks such as megalodon. It would help explain the abundance of shark tooth fossils.

In 1975, an author speculated that the Loch Ness Monster was a *Plesiosaurus* that had not gone extinct. But scientists have debunked this claim and the existence of the Loch Ness Monster.

PLESIOSAURUS

Plesiosauria is an order of marine reptiles with two branches. One branch includes smaller reptiles in the genus *Plesiosaurus*. *Plesiosaurus* lived during the Jurassic Period. *Plesiosaurus* fossils have been found throughout the world.

COMPLETING THE PICTURE

In 1823, paleontologist Mary Anning discovered the first complete skeleton of this marine reptile. This skeleton is on display at London's Natural History Museum. It has a broad body with a long neck and small skull resembling that of a snake. It also has a short tail and two pairs of large paddles. Fossils indicate *Plesiosaurus* grew to be about 15 feet (4.5 m) long. It swung its long neck from side to side to capture prey with its sharp teeth.

Plesiosaurus had nostrils far back on its head, near its eyes.

PLIOSAURS

The order Plesiosauria also includes pliosaurs. These creatures were a Jurassic relative of *Plesiosaurus*. Both types of marine reptiles had turtle-like bodies with four flippers. However, pliosaurs were much larger than *Plesiosaurus*. Few pliosaur fossils have been found. The most complete skull yet found was reported in 2023. It was discovered in a rocky cliff in

Fossils from the upper and lower jaws of a pliosaur were discovered in Dorset, United Kingdom.

England, 50 feet (15 m) aboveground. Researchers had to excavate the rock while strapped to ropes hanging over the side of the cliff.

PREDATOR X

Between 2004 and 2012, the fragments of two pliosaur skeletons were excavated on an Arctic island. The media called the animal Predator X. At first, scientists estimated this pliosaur grew to be 50 feet (15 m) long. But they later updated this estimate. Scientists now agree that Predator X, or *Pliosaurus funkei*, was closer to 40 feet (12 m) long.

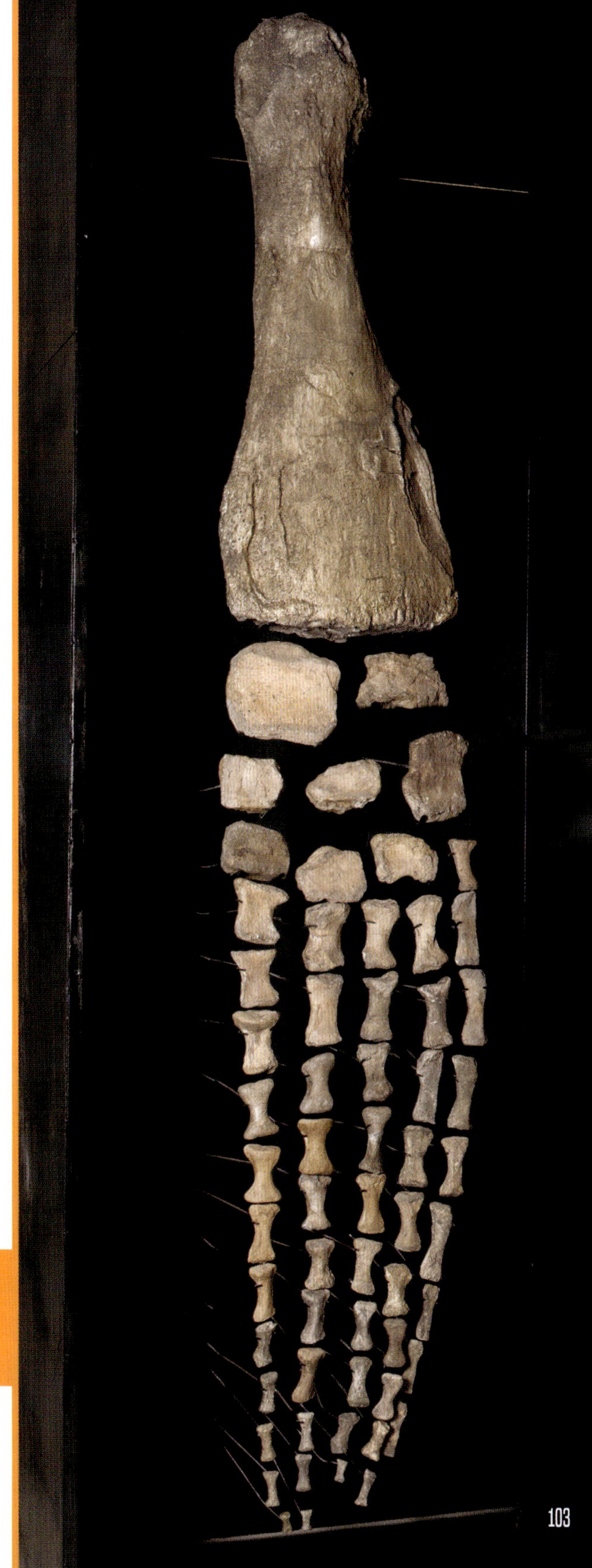

Fossilized bones from a pliosaur's paddle were found in England.

Artists have drawn the modern goblin shark. This shark likely resembled the ancient *Scapanorhynchus*.

SCAPANORHYNCHUS

Scapanorhynchus is an ancient relative of modern goblin sharks. Most fossils from this species are of only the teeth. A typical tooth is slender and shaped like a dagger. Almost no skeleton fossils have been recovered. However, goblin sharks are living fossils. These sharks have changed little over time. Scientists study living sharks to increase their understanding of extinct ones.

UNUSUAL HEAD

Scapanorhynchus, like a modern goblin shark, had a long, flat snout and tiny eyes. Beneath the snout were retractable jaws. This allowed the shark to thrust out its jaws at 10 feet (3 m) per second. The jaws returned to their original position after the prey was snatched. Modern descendants of this shark are rarely seen because they live deep in the ocean. They use electrical sensors in their snouts to track the movement of prey.

A modern goblin shark has too many teeth to fit inside its mouth, even when the mouth is closed.

TANYSTROPHEUS

Tanystropheus was a reptile that lived in shallow waters during the Mesozoic Era. Based on fossils, *Tanystropheus* had a very long neck and a body with small limbs. It grew up to 20 feet (6 m) long. In 2023, researchers published a study about a *Tanystropheus* skeleton that consists of a small head and part of a long neck. The neck bones had tooth marks. This is a sign that the neck was bitten off by a predator.

EVOLVING THEORIES

Tanystropheus is a good example of how scientific theories can evolve over time as new fossils are found and new technologies are introduced. The first *Tanystropheus* fossils were discovered in 1852. Researchers thought *Tanystropheus* was a flying dinosaur. This is because it had long, hollow bones similar to those that made up the wings of flying animals. As more fossils were found, it seemed like the long bones came from a reptile's neck. It didn't have wings.

Tanystropheus had a neck that was likely three times longer than its torso.

Some complete or nearly complete skeletons of *Tanystropheus* have been unearthed.

But scientists were then unsure whether *Tanystropheus* was a land or aquatic animal. Three-dimensional models of crushed skull pieces solved the mystery. They revealed that the reptile's nostrils were on top of its snout, like those of a crocodile. This indicates it swam but did not live underwater.

The name *Tiktaalik* came from the Indigenous Inuit language spoken near the first fossil's discovery site in Canada. It means "large, shallow-water fish."

TIKTAALIK

Tiktaalik lived during the Paleozoic Era. It had features of both a fish and a tetrapod. The first *Tiktaalik* fossils were discovered on Canada's Ellesmere Island in 2004. Researchers created a skeletal reconstruction of *Tiktaalik* using CT scanners. The resulting three-dimensional image showed that *Tiktaalik* had the fins, scales, and gills of a fish. It lived in water. But its

wide, flat skull resembled a crocodile's head. It had four limbs with wristbones. It also had a neck and shoulders, a pelvis, and thick ribs similar to those often found in tetrapods.

Tiktaalik is a transitional fossil. It shows how animals evolved to live on land. *Tiktaalik* fossils date back to 375 million years ago. Some of these animals grew to about 9 feet (2.7 m) long.

The pelvis of *Tiktaalik* shows that although the hind limbs resembled fins, the animal could likely use these limbs to walk.

FINDING *TIKTAALIK*

Spotting: In 2004, paleontologists in the Arctic Circle noticed an impression in the rock. It looked like the snout of a fish-like creature.

Digging: Researchers dug out several pieces of rock that contained fossils of the same creature. These rocks were taken to laboratories.

Unearthing: Experts used special tools and chemicals to slowly remove the sediment surrounding the fossil.

Scanning: CT scans of the fossils created three-dimensional images. These images showed the inside of the skull, vertebrae, and ribs.

Researching: In 2006, scientists announced their findings. *Tiktaalik* is a link in the fish-to-tetrapod transition.

Artistic re-creation of organism
Wide, flat skull
Limbs with wristbones
Organism's land and marine habitat

XIPHACTINUS

Xiphactinus was a giant bony fish from the Mesozoic Era. The first *Xiphactinus* fossils were discovered in 1870. Since then, many complete fossils of this fish have been found worldwide. Twelve nearly complete skeletons were recovered in Kansas alone. Several skeletons had fossils of large, undigested fish inside them. One of these fish-in-a-fish fossils is now on display at the Sternberg Museum of Natural History in Kansas.

Xiphactinus likely used the fangs at the front of its jaw to impale prey when it attacked.

In 1926, workers from the Smithsonian Institution mounted a complete *Xiphactinus* skeleton, along with a large fish that was found inside the predator's stomach.

BULLDOG FISH

Xiphactinus likely had a long, sleek body. It grew to be about 16 to 20 feet (4.8 to 6 m) long. It had fang-like teeth. The lower jaw jutted ahead of its eyes. This earned it the nickname "bulldog fish." It was a generalist predator. This means it ate almost any marine animal that it found.

DID YOU KNOW?

Fossils can be found in many ways. Most people dig for them. But a fisherman hooked a 90-million-year-old fish fossil in a Nebraska river. It turned out to be a fossilized *Xiphactinus*.

Allosaurus teeth were curved backward to keep prey trapped in its mouth.

ALLOSAURUS

Allosaurus was a theropod that lived between 150 and 144 million years ago. Theropods were dinosaurs that walked on two legs and had short arms. Many were carnivores.

The bones from about 50 different *Allosaurus* skeletons have been unearthed at the Cleveland-Lloyd Dinosaur Quarry in Utah. These are some of more than 12,000 bones from at least 74 Jurassic animals found there. The ground may have been sticky at this site, trapping animals and attracting predators. It may also have been an area with an important water source. The Natural History Museum of Utah has the most complete collection of *Allosaurus* fossils in the world.

GIANT PREDATOR

Scientists have been able to reconstruct a skeleton of *Allosaurus* based on the discovered fossils. *Allosaurus* grew about 35 feet (10.7 m) long. Its tail made up half its body length. It had three-fingered hands with claws. Short horns grew above its eyes.

WHAT WERE DINOSAURS?

Dinosaurs were reptiles that lived during the Mesozoic Era. But unlike modern reptiles, their legs grew straight under their bodies. As a result, dinosaurs had an upright stance. The legs of reptiles such as lizards and crocodiles grow out from the sides of their bodies. They have a sprawling stance.

Trace fossils of *Allosaurus* tracks have been preserved in Utah.

ANKYLOSAURUS

Ankylosaurus was the largest of the ankylosaurs. These were armored dinosaurs that lived between 68 and 66 million years ago. *Ankylosaurus* fossils have been found in the United States and Canada. They were first excavated in 1906 at the Hell Creek Formation in Montana. Since then, researchers have found fossilized skulls, plates, club tails, bone fragments, and footprints. But they have not uncovered a complete skeleton.

CRETACEOUS TANK

Scientists look to the fossils of other ankylosaurs to help them understand *Ankylosaurus*. *Ankylosaurus* was a herbivore that walked on four legs. *Ankylosaurus* has been called the living tank of the Cretaceous. It was the size of a military tank at about 30 feet (9 m) long. *Ankylosaurus* weighed almost 18,000 pounds (8,160 kg). It had rows of spiked armor joined by a bony covering. Its tail ended in a large, heavy club that it used to fight predators.

Researchers have uncovered fossilized skin from several species of ankylosaurs.

More complete fossils from *Gastonia burgei*, another ankylosaur, show similarities to *Ankylosaurus*, including plated armor.

A detailed, nearly complete *Archaeopteryx* fossil was preserved in a plate of limestone. This fossil was critical to scientific study of the dinosaur.

ARCHAEOPTERYX

Archaeopteryx was a small dinosaur with feathers. It lived about 150 million years ago. The first *Archaeopteryx* fossil was discovered in the 1860s.

A complete skeleton was found in the Solnhofen Limestone in Germany. This fossil shows that *Archaeopteryx* had traits of a dinosaur, including teeth, clawed fingers, and a long, bony tail. But it also shows features of a modern bird, such as wings, feathers, and a wishbone.

DINOSAUR OR BIRD?

The excavation of more *Archaeopteryx* fossils sparked a scientific debate. Experts wonder whether this animal was a bird or a dinosaur. Some say it was a flightless dinosaur with feathers. Others think it was a true bird that could fly in bursts. Modern birds descended from dinosaurs. *Archaeopteryx* may represent an evolutionary transition from dinosaurs to birds.

Archaeopteryx was about the size of a pigeon.

ARGENTINOSAURUS

Argentinosaurus belongs to the group of sauropods known as titanosaurs. Sauropods were huge, herbivorous dinosaurs that had small heads with long necks and tails. They had four pillar-like legs. Titanosaurs were a group of sauropods known to be some of the largest dinosaurs ever discovered.

Argentinosaurus lived 90 million years ago in what is now the Patagonia region of Argentina. This is an area where other titanosaurs have been discovered. Few *Argentinosaurus* fossils have been found. So far, researchers have unearthed only a few leg, pelvis, and vertebrae bones. One vertebra was more than 5 feet (1.5 m) tall and 4 feet (1.2 m) wide. A full-size replica of *Argentinosaurus* is displayed at the Museo Municipal Carmen Funes in Argentina.

GIANT AMONG GIANTS

To reconstruct *Argentinosaurus*, scientists looked to fossils of other sauropods. *Argentinosaurus* was about 123 feet (37 m) long. That is approximately the length of four school buses. It may have weighed as much as 150,000 pounds (68,000 kg).

Argentinosaurus is the largest land animal ever discovered.

A cast of an *Argentinosaurus* vertebra is displayed in Los Angeles's Natural History Museum. The vertebrae of this dinosaur could reach up to 5 feet (1.5 m) in height.

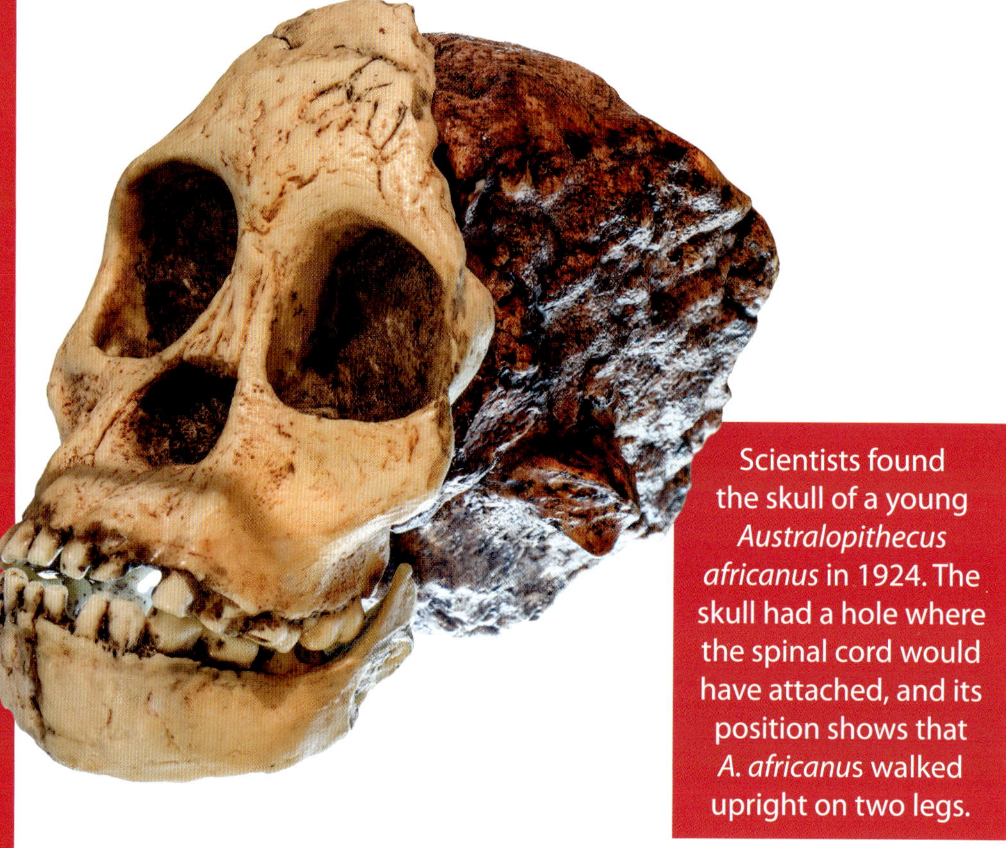

Scientists found the skull of a young *Australopithecus africanus* in 1924. The skull had a hole where the spinal cord would have attached, and its position shows that *A. africanus* walked upright on two legs.

AUSTRALOPITHECUS

Australopithecus was a member of the Hominini group. Hominins were early ancestors of modern humans. In 1974, the most complete *Australopithecus* skeleton was discovered in Ethiopia. The fossil was three million years old.

Scientists studied the skeleton's teeth, legs, and pelvis to conclude the *Australopithecus* was a female hominin. She was nicknamed "Lucy." Lucy was between 12 and 18 years old. Her brain cavity was much smaller than that of a human. This suggests that primates evolved to walk on two legs before they evolved to have the large brains of modern humans.

THE LAETOLI FOOTPRINTS

In 1978, three sets of fossilized footprints were discovered in Tanzania. The footprints look as though people walked barefoot through cement. In fact, they walked in wet volcanic ash.

After the imprints were made, more ash covered and preserved the footprints as trace fossils. The trail of footprints is nearly 90 feet (27 m) long and about four million years old. This trail is named the Laetoli footprints. These trace fossils suggest that hominins such as *Australopithecus* walked fully upright and near one another.

The skeleton of Lucy is about 40 percent complete. It includes bones from the arms, legs, spine, and pelvis. Scientists have reconstructed a skull based on the lower jawbone, which was also fossilized.

BRACHIOSAURUS

Brachiosaurus was a sauropod that lived in what is now North America between 156 and 151 million years ago. The first *Brachiosaurus* fossil, a skull, was found in Colorado in 1883. At first, it was wrongly categorized as a *Brontosaurus* skull. Scientists recategorized the skull as a *Brachiosaurus* in 1998.

Only ten *Brachiosaurus* fossils have ever been found, and none have shown a complete skeleton. Scientists do not know why *Brachiosaurus* fossils are so rare. Hundreds of fossils belonging to other sauropods have been excavated. One theory is that *Brachiosaurus* lived in an environment that did not have the right conditions for creating fossils.

A *Brachiosaurus* skull shows that the dinosaur had a small, bony crest on top of its head.

A researcher lay next to a *Brachiosaurus* leg bone after the fossil was discovered.

BIG APPETITE

Scientists studied the fossils of *Giraffatitan*, a close relative, to learn about *Brachiosaurus*. Connections between the fossils suggest *Brachiosaurus* was about 82 feet (25 m) long and weighed about 176,000 pounds (79,800 kg). It may have eaten up to 880 pounds (400 kg) of plant matter every day.

JURASSIC PARK APPEARANCE

A full-size reconstruction of *Brachiosaurus* went on display at the Field Museum in Chicago, Illinois, in 1994. This was the year after the sauropod appeared in the hit film *Jurassic Park*. The skeleton stood in the museum's entrance hall. But it was later moved and is now on display at Chicago's O'Hare International Airport.

Ceratosaurus had sharp teeth. It was a fierce predator that likely preyed on other dinosaurs and aquatic animals.

CERATOSAURUS

Ceratosaurus was a Jurassic theropod. Its name means "horned lizard" in Greek. The first *Ceratosaurus* skeleton was discovered in 1883 in Colorado. Researchers cut out the rock around the dinosaur. The huge slab was eventually shipped to the National Museum of Natural History in Washington, DC. The museum decided to display the dinosaur still in the rock. In 1911, the rock-encased *Ceratosaurus* became part of a wall in the museum's Fossil Hall. The *Ceratosaurus* stayed there for more than 100 years. Then, in 2014, the museum decided to free it from the rock. It took experts more than a year to chisel away the hard sandstone without damaging the bones.

NEW INFORMATION

Paleontologists were excited to have better access to the *Ceratosaurus* skeleton. Few other *Ceratosaurus* fossils have been found. This skeleton provides scientists with more information about the theropod. Its fossilized skull shows several horns, including on its nose and above its eyes. Armor covered its back. The dinosaur's teeth were sharp. These traits show it was a fierce predator.

A nearly complete *Ceratosaurus* skeleton was found in the Morrison Formation in the western United States. The fossils are part of the Natural History Museum of Utah's collection.

COELODONTA

Coelodonta is an extinct genus known as the woolly rhinoceros. Many well-preserved *Coelodonta* fossils exist. Frozen, mummified carcasses have been found in the region of Siberia in Asia. One was discovered in 2024, helping scientists continue to learn about this genus.

Ancient rhinoceroses were also embalmed in oil seeps and tar. Researchers have found preserved carcasses with soft tissue intact. Humans may have hunted these animals.

Coelodonta had two large horns.

Coelodonta had long hair that kept out the snow and wind in its cold habitat.

Drawings of woolly rhinoceroses are on the walls of the Chauvet–Pont d'Arc cave in France, dating back 30,000 years.

Scientists have compared *Coelodonta* fossils to modern rhinoceroses to learn about this extinct species. *Coelodonta* was likely a herbivore that lived in the cold regions of Asia, North Africa, and Europe. It had a long nose horn with a smaller horn behind it. Scientists have debated why this animal became extinct. Climate change and human hunting may have been factors.

Scientists carefully cleaned the *Coelophysis* fossils discovered at Ghost Ranch in 1990.

COELOPHYSIS

Coelophysis was one of the earliest dinosaurs. This small theropod lived in what is now the western United States between 225 and 190 million years ago. Hundreds of *Coelophysis* skeletons have been found in a New Mexico quarry called Ghost Ranch.

Ghost Ranch is now a desert but was once a marsh with giant rivers. Water or a food source brought many dinosaurs to this area. Then a flash flood drowned and buried them quickly with moving sediment. Some of the found *Coelophysis* skeletons had their last meals in their stomachs, including a small crocodile. A bronze cast of a *Coelophysis* skeleton is on the wall at the 81st Street subway station in New York City. This is the stop for the American Museum of Natural History.

EARLY THEROPOD

Fossils suggest *Coelophysis* was about 10 feet (3 m) long. It lived before dinosaurs became apex predators. But its anatomy suggests why some theropods evolved into predators that ruled the Jurassic world. *Coelophysis* had sharp claws and sharp teeth. It ran quickly on two legs.

Hollow bones made *Coelophysis* a light and fast hunter. In fact, its name means "hollow form."

DEINONYCHUS

Deinonychus was a theropod that lived between 146 and 100 million years ago. It was a member of the group commonly called raptors. The first *Deinonychus* fossils were discovered by American paleontologist John Ostrom. They were found in 1964 in Montana's badlands, a dry region with little vegetation.

Ostrom excavated more than 1,000 bones belonging to *Deinonychus*. He then assembled a skeleton that revolutionized the study of dinosaurs. Previously, scientists thought all dinosaurs were slow-moving giants. But this skeleton showed a medium-sized dinosaur with long legs and light bones. These are signs of speed.

Deinonychus was about 8 feet (2.4 m) long.

Deinonychus likely had feathers, although none have been fossilized.

DESIGNED TO HUNT

Ostrom's fossils also showed that *Deinonychus* was a predator. Its name means "terrible claw." This is a reference to the giant curved claw on its second toe. Its large jaws were filled with sharp teeth that curved backward to hold on to prey.

BIRD BONES

Ostrom noticed that the hands, arms, legs, and feet of *Deinonychus* were similar to those of modern birds. In particular, *Deinonychus* and birds have a special wristbone called the semilunate carpal. This bone allows the wrist to bend so the fingers lie close to the forearm. This was some of the first evidence that birds are descended from theropod dinosaurs.

Scientists are not sure how *Dilophosaurus* used its crests. They may have helped the dinosaur attract a mate.

DILOPHOSAURUS

Dilophosaurus was a meat-eating theropod dinosaur that roamed what is now North America 184 million years ago. Jesse Williams discovered the first *Dilophosaurus* fossils in 1940. He was a member of the Navajo Nation and found the fossils on Navajo land at the Kayenta Formation in Arizona.

Paleontologist Sam Welles thought the bones belonged to a species of *Megalosaurus*. Ten years later, Welles found fossils of the same dinosaur showing head crests. He realized these fossils were from a new species of carnivorous dinosaur. He named it *Dilophosaurus*. *Dilophosaurus* means "double-crested lizard." It was named for two crests on its skull that extended from its nostrils to its eyes.

JURASSIC PARK MISTAKES

Dilophosaurus appeared in the 1993 movie *Jurassic Park*. However, the fictionalized dinosaur was not entirely accurate. For example, *Dilophosaurus* did not have neck frills that expanded like two giant fans, which the movie showed. But *Jurassic Park* did follow science in other ways. It showed *Dilophosaurus* as fast, clever, and bird-like.

Artists have created images of *Dilophosaurus, shown*, that are more accurate than its portrayal in *Jurassic Park*. In reality, the dinosaur was twice as large as the movie's version.

DIMETRODON

Dimetrodon resembled a dinosaur. But it became extinct about 270 million years ago. This was long before dinosaurs appeared. The first *Dimetrodon* fossil was found in Canada in 1845. It was named *Bathygnathus* and grouped with dinosaurs.

However, additional discoveries showed scientists that the fossils were older than those of dinosaurs. Features of the animal's skull proved it was not a reptile. After learning

Paleontologists from the Houston Museum of Natural Science unearthed new *Dimetrodon* fossils in 2010.

A *Dimetrodon* skeleton is displayed at the Royal Tyrrell Museum in Alberta, Canada.

it was not a dinosaur, scientists changed the animal's name to *Dimetrodon*. They grouped it with synapsids, which are early relatives of mammals. Humans are more closely related to *Dimetrodon* than dinosaurs are. A full skeleton of *Dimetrodon* is on display at the American Museum of Natural History.

SAIL ON

This predator had a thick body and four short limbs. Fossils show that it was about 12 feet (3.7 m) in length, including its long tail. Its large skull was filled with sharp teeth.

The most distinctive feature of *Dimetrodon* is the sail on its back. The sail is made of long, bony rods that rise into the air from its spine. These have been fossilized. The sail would have been covered with skin. However, the skin is not preserved in fossils.

A cleaner dusts a *Diplodocus* skeleton replica displayed at the Natural History Museum in London.

DIPLODOCUS

Diplodocus was one of the longest sauropods ever at 100 feet (30 m). It lived between 161 and 146 million years ago. Researchers have uncovered the skeletons of an entire herd of this dinosaur. They have even found skin impressions in stone. Many fossils were discovered at the Mother's Day Quarry in Montana. The quarry is part of the fossil-rich Morrison

Formation that runs from New Mexico to Canada.

"DIPPY"

The Carnegie Museum of Natural History in Pittsburgh, Pennsylvania, has a complete *Diplodocus* skeleton nicknamed "Dippy." Andrew Carnegie funded the expeditions that led to the discovery of this skeleton in 1899. He built a room called the Dinosaur Hall to display it. People flocked to see this creature. Scientists re-created Dippy's skeleton. The re-creations were displayed at museums around the world.

DID YOU KNOW?

In 1902, King Edward VII of England toured Carnegie's home in Scotland and saw a picture of *Diplodocus*. He wanted one for England. Carnegie replicated Dippy in plaster and sent it to London.

Diplodocus was a herbivore with rows of comb-like teeth.

EDMONTOSAURUS

Edmontosaurus was a Cretaceous member of the hadrosaurs, known as duck-billed dinosaurs. This nickname refers to hadrosaurs' flat snouts. An abundance of *Edmontosaurus* fossils have been found on nearly every continent. *Edmontosaurus* was prey for *Tyrannosaurus rex*, shown by fossilized *T. rex* bite marks on *Edmontosaurus* bones. Fossils also show *Edmontosaurus* had a small, comb-like structure on its head.

Edmontosaurus skeletons are so plentiful that some people call hadrosaurs the caribou of the Cretaceous.

Rows of teeth preserved as fossils show that *Edmontosaurus* was a herbivore that chewed tough plants.

PRESERVED SKIN

Edmontosaurus remains have been found with their skins preserved. This is a rare type of fossil. Most soft tissue, such as skin, is preserved through mummification. But the *Edmontosaurus* skin had turned to stone, not into a mummy.

Mummies are created in two ways. Either the organism had a quick burial, or dry air preserved it. *Edmontosaurus* skin was not mummified. But scientists realized soft tissue could be preserved another way. They studied an *Edmontosaurus* with bite marks. These bites allowed gas and liquid to escape the corpse. This exposed the inside of the skin and allowed it to dry out enough to be preserved. The corpse was then covered in sediment, and permineralization began.

Fossils from *Fona herzogae* are displayed at the North Carolina Museum of Natural Sciences.

FONA HERZOGAE

In 2024, researchers in Utah discovered the skeletal remains of a new species of dinosaur. They came across small bones in several burrows. Many of the skeletons were complete and in good condition. A flood likely covered the area. Being underground killed the dinosaurs but preserved their remains.

The species was named *Fona herzogae*. A researcher chose the name to honor a spirit, Fo'na, in a creation myth from Guam. In the myth, Fo'na helps create the universe. When she dies, people are born from her fossils.

GOOD DIGGERS

Fossils of small dinosaurs are rare because these animals were easy prey. Their delicate bones were often destroyed before they could become fossils. The fossilization process of *F. herzogae* gave scientists many well-preserved fossils to research.

F. herzogae was a herbivore that lived about 99 million years ago. It was the size of a large dog. It had sturdy hips, wide shoulders, and strong arm muscles used for digging.

F. herzogae is one of very few burrowing dinosaurs ever discovered. These animals may have lived partly underground or used their dens as safe spaces to hide or raise young. Burrows could have provided shelter from predators and most dangerous weather.

GIGANOTOSAURUS

Giganotosaurus was a huge Cretaceous theropod. Amateur fossil hunter Rubén Carolini discovered the first *Giganotosaurus* bones in 1993. Carolini was a car mechanic who was searching for fossils in his spare time. He found *Giganotosaurus* in the Candeleros Formation in Argentina. The skeleton was 70 percent complete. The species *Giganotosaurus carolinii* is named after him.

A replica of *Giganotosaurus* is on display at the Australian Museum in Sydney, Australia. It shows a huge skull with sharp, saw-like teeth for slicing through prey. *Giganotosaurus* had a small brain for its size.

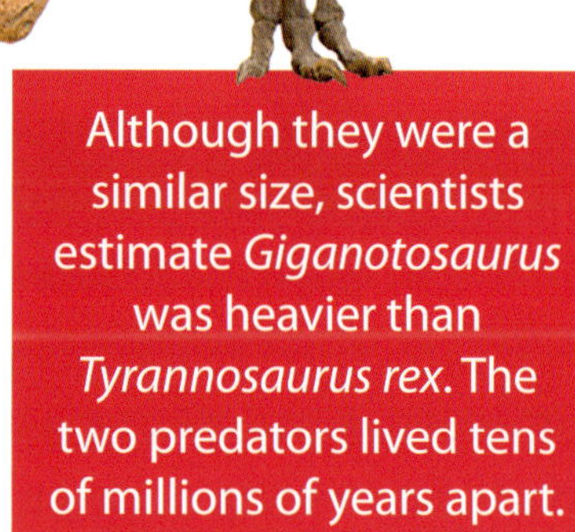

Although they were a similar size, scientists estimate *Giganotosaurus* was heavier than *Tyrannosaurus rex*. The two predators lived tens of millions of years apart.

UPDATING THE RECORD

Scientific measures of extinct species can change as new fossils are found. This is what happened when a new *Giganotosaurus* jawbone

Giganotosaurus carolinii is the only species of *Giganotosaurus.*

was discovered. It was 8 percent larger than the one found on Carolini's dinosaur. Experts increased their size and weight estimates based on this new find. This giant theropod could grow up to 42 feet (13 m) long. *Giganotosaurus* could run 31 miles per hour (50 kmh).

Giganotosaurus had many teeth. They grew up to about 8 inches (20 cm) long.

MAMMUTHUS PRIMIGENIUS

Mammuthus primigenius, or the woolly mammoth, was a furry relative of the modern Asian elephant. It lived mostly near the Arctic between 700,000 and 4,000 years ago. The carcasses of several mummified mammoths have been discovered. These fossils had been preserved in frozen ground. The mummies have provided scientists with a great deal of information about the woolly mammoth.

Like today's elephants, *Mammuthus primigenius* was a four-legged herbivore with a trunk. It had long, curved tusks made of ivory. It had several features that helped it survive freezing weather. These included long hair that covered its body and trunk. It also had a thick layer of fat for insulation.

The Seodaemun Museum of Natural History in Seoul, South Korea, displayed a *Mammuthus primigenius* skeleton alongside a re-creation of the living animal.

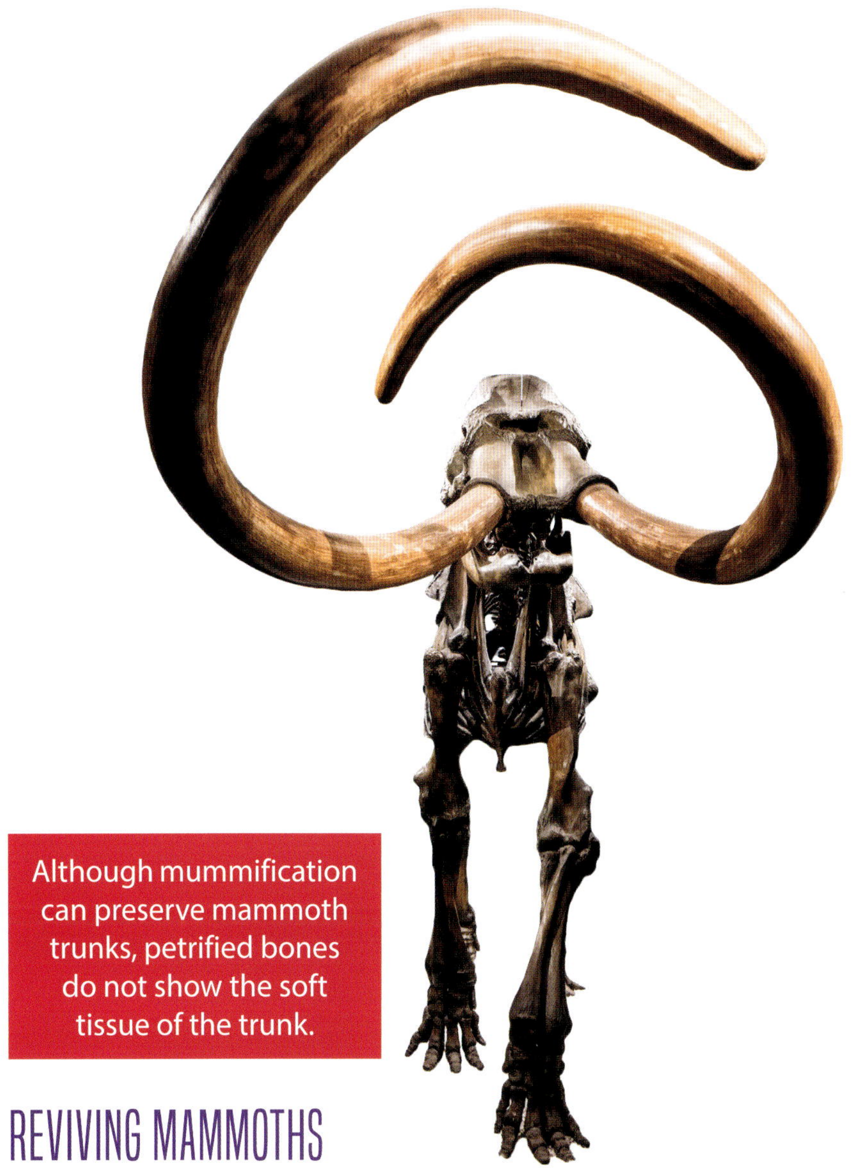

Although mummification can preserve mammoth trunks, petrified bones do not show the soft tissue of the trunk.

REVIVING MAMMOTHS

Deoxyribonucleic acid (DNA) has been extracted from mammoth mummies. DNA is a chemical that is the basis of genetics. It shows how an organism develops and functions. Some scientists are experimenting with using DNA to bring the woolly mammoth back from extinction. They plan to use elephant DNA to fill in any gaps in the mammoth DNA extracted from fossils. Then scientists would use a process called cloning to produce an *M. primigenius* embryo.

Marks on fossilized teeth from *Megaloceros giganteus* show that the deer was a herbivore.

MEGALOCEROS GIGANTEUS

Megaloceros giganteus was a giant deer often called the Irish elk. *M. giganteus* lived during the Cenozoic Era, from about 400,000 to 8,000 years ago. Many fossils have been found in Ireland's peat bogs. Peat bogs are wetlands filled with rotting plant matter. They are good for preserving remains because they have no oxygen to speed the decaying process. *M. giganteus* fossils have also been discovered in Europe, Asia, and North Africa. This species has been compared to an elk or moose because of its antlers. But fossils show the Irish elk had much larger antlers than modern moose.

SHOULDERING THE WEIGHT

M. giganteus antlers could grow 13 feet across (4 m) and weigh more than 110 pounds (50 kg). Fossils show that these animals had thick skulls and strong bones in their necks. Long vertebrae suggest males had a hump of muscles in their backs. These adaptations allowed males to carry such large, heavy antlers.

Some *M. giganteus* remains were likely covered by sediment from melting glaciers, allowing for their fossilization.

MEGALOSAURUS

Megalosaurus was the first scientific name ever given to a dinosaur based on its fossils. Geologist William Buckland came up with the name in 1824. Buckland thought he was identifying the remains of a giant lizard that he'd found in England. Based on its fossils, he thought the animal was the height of an elephant and the length of a whale.

SIZE DEBATE

More than 200 years later, researchers are still debating what *Megalosaurus* looked like. This is because very few of this dinosaur's fossils have been recovered. From what little has been found, experts theorize it was a theropod that was 20 feet (6 m) long. It lived about 168 million years ago.

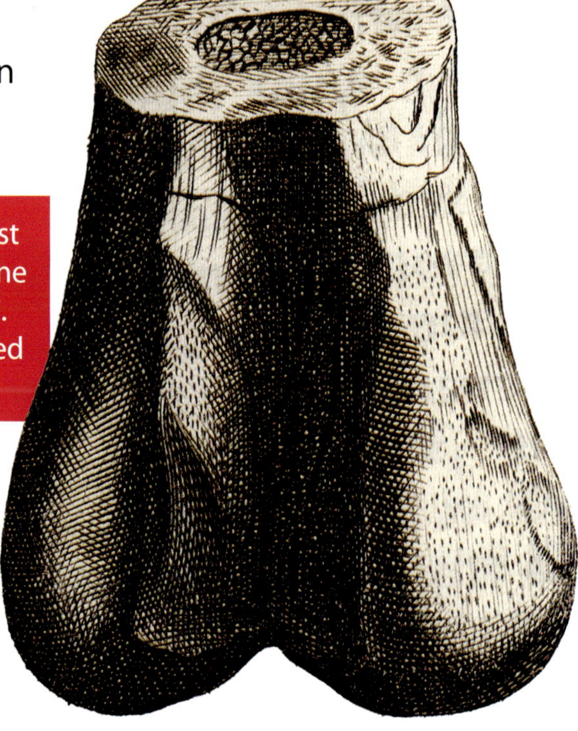

An illustration of the first discovered dinosaur bone was published in 1677. This fossil likely belonged to *Megalosaurus*.

The Oxford University Museum of Natural History displays casts of *Megalosaurus* footprints on its lawn.

Microraptor is the smallest dinosaur found to date.

MICRORAPTOR

Microraptor was a small, feathered theropod with wings. The discovery of the first *Microraptor* was announced in 2003. Since then, about 300 fossils of *Microraptor* have been found in China.

Paleontologists were surprised to learn that *Microraptor* had long flight feathers on both its arms and its legs. This meant it had four wings. This was unlike other flying dinosaurs that had only two wings. The fossils show that it was the size of a crow and weighed less than 3 pounds (1.4 kg).

DID YOU KNOW?

In 1999, *National Geographic* announced the discovery of a winged dinosaur called *Archaeoraptor*. But it turned out the person who claimed to find *Archaeoraptor* was pulling a hoax. He had added the tail of a *Microraptor* to the body of a different dinosaur.

FOSSILIZED COLORS

Few animal pigments have been discovered that survived the fossilization process. However, in 2012, pigment cells called melanosomes were found in fossilized *Microraptor* feathers. Scientists used a powerful microscope to determine that the theropod had glossy black feathers.

Microraptor lived 120 million years ago.

ONYCHONYCTERIS

Onychonycteris was an ancient bat that lived about 52 million years ago. Bats are the only mammals that can fly. A complete skeleton of *Onychonycteris* was discovered in 2003. It was excavated at Fossil Lake in Wyoming. The area is now a desert. But 52 million years ago, it was a deep lake. No scavengers lived in the lake. Most corpses that fell to the bottom remained untouched. Fine sediment flowed off the surrounding hills and into the lake during rainstorms. These were ideal conditions for preserving remains.

The Royal Ontario Museum has an *Onychonycteris finneyi* fossil that was found in Wyoming.

EVOLUTIONARY LINK

Onychonycteris fossils are some of the few complete bat remains that have been discovered. The species *Onychonycteris finneyi* provides an evolutionary link between modern bats and their early ancestors that did not fly. Bones suggest it could use an early form of echolocation. Modern bats use echolocation to navigate at night. This finding suggests *O. finneyi* was active during the day, since its nighttime navigation skills would have been poor.

O. finneyi had claws on its wings that allowed it to climb.

OVIRAPTOR

Oviraptor was a small theropod that ate both plants and animals. It lived during the Mesozoic Era. Like all dinosaurs, it reproduced by laying eggs. In 1993, the fossil of an *Oviraptor* egg was discovered. The shell was broken, revealing the bones of a tiny dinosaur inside. It is not unusual to unearth pieces of fossilized eggshells. But it is rare to find an intact egg. The embryo inside the fossil was about 8 inches (20 cm) long. It had all of its bones except the tail and back legs. A paleontologist found the fossil in the Gobi, a desert in Mongolia.

A museum in Germany displayed a re-creation of a fossilized *Oviraptor* embryo.

Oviraptor sat on its eggs before they hatched, much like many modern birds.

MISIDENTIFIED

The name *Oviraptor* means "egg thief." In 1923, a paleontologist discovered an *Oviraptor* skeleton on top of fossilized eggs. He believed the eggs belonged to the dinosaur *Protoceratops* and *Oviraptor* was stealing them. But the egg discovered in 1993 matched those found in 1923. The earlier identification of *Protoceratops* had been incorrect. *Oviraptor* had been sitting on its own eggs. This discovery proved that *Oviraptor* was a protective parent, not an egg thief.

A *Parasaurolophus* skeleton is displayed at the Royal Ontario Museum.

PARASAUROLOPHUS

Parasaurolophus was a Cretaceous hadrosaur. It lived between 77 and 73 million years ago. It was a dinosaur with a thick body and long, heavy tail. The back legs are longer than the front legs. Hadrosaurs could likely walk on two legs but mostly stayed on all four. The first fossils of *Parasaurolophus* were found in Canada in 1920.

HORN BLOWER

Parasaurolophus is best known for the giant crest on its head. Fossils show that the crest started at its nose and extended past the back of its head. The crest could be as long as 5 feet (1.5 m).

Scientists used computers to re-create the head of *Parasaurolophus* from a skull fossil. They discovered that the giant crest could make sounds similar to those of a trumpet. *Parasaurolophus* probably lived in herds. These sounds might have helped the animals communicate with one another. The crest also may have been used to help *Parasaurolophus* find a mate, warn of dangers, or be recognized by others.

A hollow tube ran through the crest of *Parasaurolophus*. It extended from the nostrils, through the crest, and back to the skull.

PHORUSRHACOS

Phorusrhacos was a member of the Phorusrhacidae family, known as terror birds. These carnivorous, flightless birds were the apex predators of their time. *Phorusrhacos* lived 12 million years ago.

Almost all fossils of terror birds have been found in Argentina. Argentinian paleontologists Florentino Ameghino and Carlos Ameghino found the first *Phorusrhacos* fossil in 1887. But the men only sketched and described its crushed skull. They left the skull in the rock because of its poor condition.

Phorusrhacos had a hook-shaped beak. This shape is seen in modern carnivorous birds.

Although *Phorusrhacos* had wings, they were underdeveloped and small.

FOSSILIZED HUNTER

Almost 100 years would pass before another skull was found. The new fossils showed *Phorusrhacos* might have used its beak to kill in two ways. The first was to snatch up its prey and throw it hard against the ground. This would break the prey's bones and make it easier to swallow. The second way was for *Phorusrhacos* to hit the prey with its beak until the animal died.

Phorusrhacos was about 8 feet (2.4 m) tall. It weighed about 300 pounds (136 kg). This is roughly the same size as a male ostrich. *Phorusrhacos* was fast even though it could not fly. It had sharp claws and a large head with a giant hooked beak.

Scientists have reconstructed the skull of *Proconsul* based on skull fragments and one complete fossil that was distorted during the permineralization process.

PROCONSUL

Proconsul is a very early primate. This omnivore lived in the tropical forests of what is now Africa during the Cenozoic Era. Fossil fragments of *Proconsul* were found in Kenya in 1927. In 1948, scientist Mary Leakey found a skull and part of a skeleton. These discoveries helped expand interest in the study of primate fossils.

MONKEY OR APE?

Evidence from fossils suggests that *Proconsul* was 3 to 5 feet (1 to 1.5 m) tall. It walked on all fours and had graceful hands. These are features of a monkey. But like apes, it did not have a tail. Its elbow anatomy may not have allowed it to swing from branch to branch. This anatomy matches that of modern apes. *Proconsul* was likely related to an ancestor of apes.

CHOOSING NAMES

There are no rules for choosing a fossil's name. Fossils are often named after the places where they were discovered or the people who found them. *Proconsul* was named after a pair of popular circus chimpanzees, both named Consul.

Proconsul lived about 17 million years ago.

PROTOCERATOPS

Protoceratops was a plant-eating dinosaur that lived in China and Mongolia. It lived about 80 million years ago. Many *Protoceratops* skeletons have been found near one another in the Gobi desert. They range in age from juvenile to adult. This abundance of skeletons has led to *Protoceratops* being called the sheep of the Cretaceous. The fossil evidence suggests that hundreds of *Protoceratops* roamed together in herds.

FIGHTING DINOSAURS

In 1971, researchers discovered the skeletons of a *Protoceratops* and a *Velociraptor* together. The *Velociraptor* is digging its toe claw into the *Protoceratops*'s neck. The *Protoceratops* had bitten

Protoceratops was similar in size and weight to a modern hog.

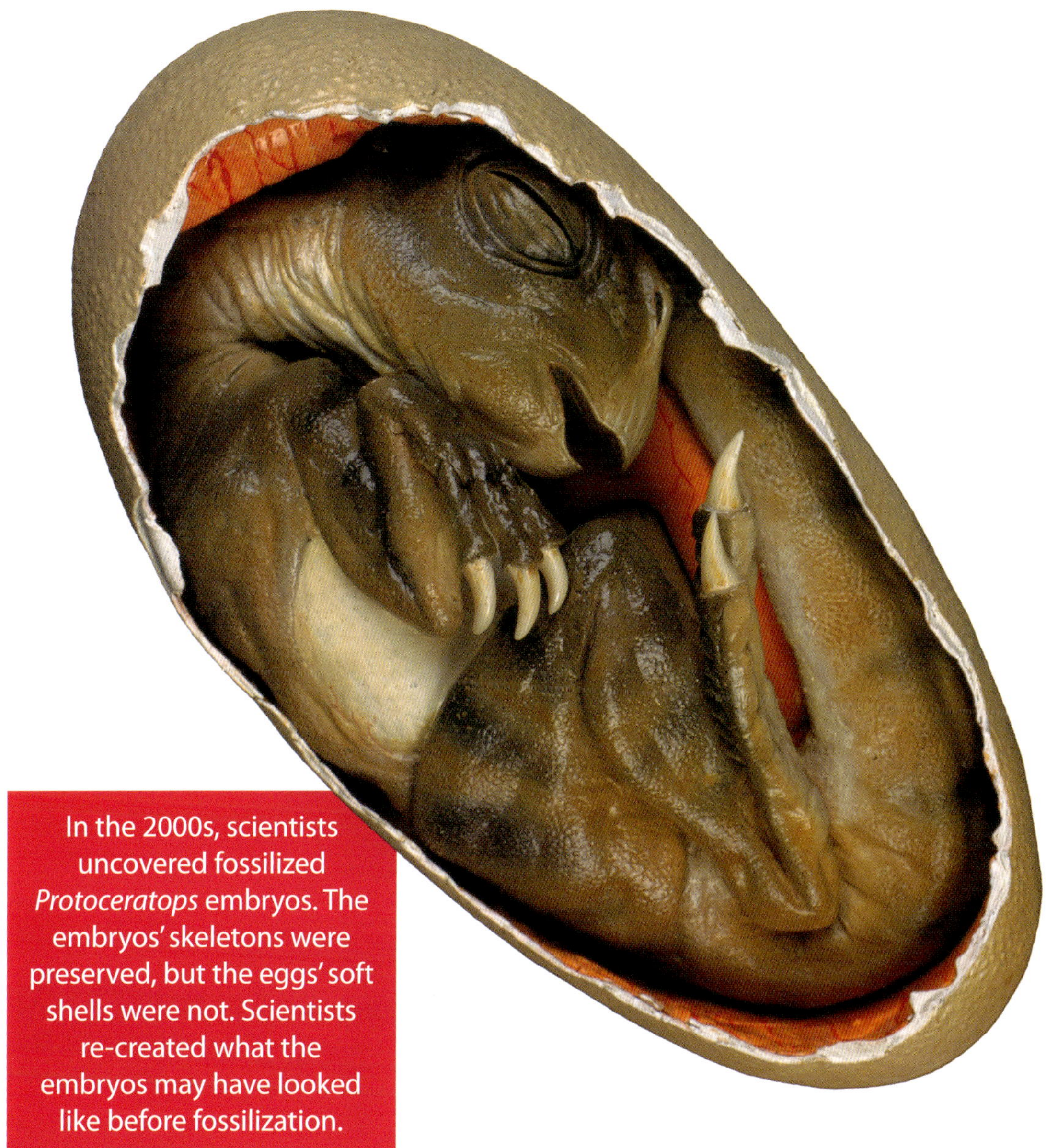

In the 2000s, scientists uncovered fossilized *Protoceratops* embryos. The embryos' skeletons were preserved, but the eggs' soft shells were not. Scientists re-created what the embryos may have looked like before fossilization.

the *Velociraptor*'s arm and broken it. These dinosaurs were preserved while fighting. One theory is that a sand dune fell on them mid-fight. This theory is supported by the S curve of the neck of the *Velociraptor*. The dinosaur's neck muscles would have been relaxed and straight if the *Velociraptor* was dead before it was buried.

All pterosaurs had long, thin beaks.

PTEROSAURS

Pterosaurs were flying reptiles. They filled the sky around the world during the Mesozoic Era. The first pterosaur fossil was discovered in the Solnhofen Limestone of Germany in about 1784. But pterosaur fossils are rare. Their hollow bones were fragile. Their corpses became fossilized only if they ended up in places with no predators or scavengers. The most complete fossils come from areas that were once filled with lagoons.

Even after fossilization, pterosaur bones could be easily damaged during excavation.

SIMILAR AND DIFFERENT

Although pterosaur fossils are rare, there is evidence of more than 100 types of pterosaurs. The size of pterosaurs varied widely. For example, the genus *Quetzalcoatlus* had a wingspan of up to 36 feet (11 m). By contrast, the wingspan of *Rhamphorhynchus* was only 3 feet (1 m).

A *Rhamphorhynchus* skeleton was preserved in a stone slab.

SINRAPTOR

Despite its name, *Sinraptor* was not a raptor or related to raptors. It was a theropod related to *Allosaurus*. It lived between 169 and 142 million years ago in China. Researchers rarely discover *Sinraptor* fossils. But the skeletons they have found have been nearly complete.

A *Sinraptor* skull is displayed in the Shanghai Natural History Museum in China.

Scientists have identified two species of *Sinraptor*.

One skeleton was found at the Shishugou Formation in China. A full-size model of this dinosaur can be seen at the Institute of Vertebrate Paleontology and Paleoanthropology in Beijing, China. *Sinraptor dongi* was named for Chinese paleontologist Dong Zhiming.

APEX PREDATOR

According to fossil evidence, *Sinraptor* was approximately 26 feet (8 m) long. In Asia, only the theropod *Yangchuanosaurus* was larger. But *Sinraptor* was found in sediment that is several million years older than that where *Yangchuanosaurus* was buried. So these two dinosaurs probably did not live at the same time. That would make *Sinraptor* the apex predator of its period.

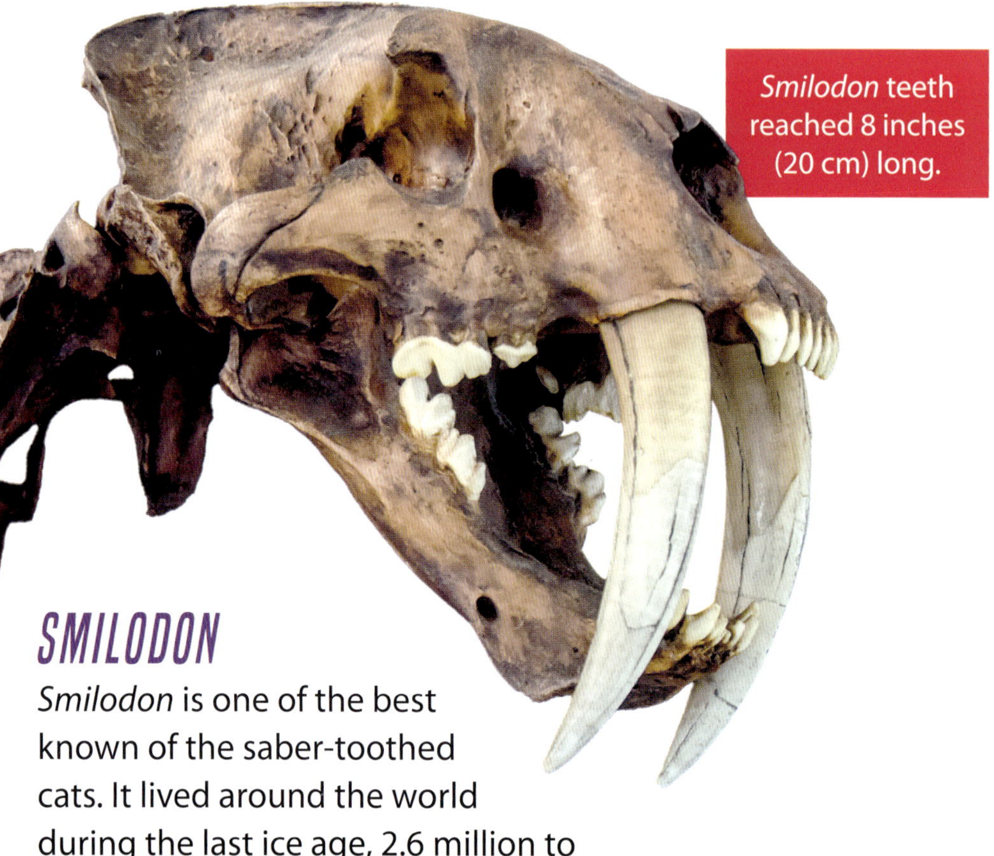

Smilodon teeth reached 8 inches (20 cm) long.

SMILODON

Smilodon is one of the best known of the saber-toothed cats. It lived around the world during the last ice age, 2.6 million to 12,000 years ago. An ice age is a geological period during which much of the land is covered with thick sheets of ice.

Smilodon remains are the second-most-common fossils discovered at the La Brea Tar Pits in Los Angeles, California. Scientists have recovered hundreds of thousands of *Smilodon* bones there. These remains show that *Smilodon* had a short tail, which suggests it did not chase prey. Cats such as cheetahs use their long tails for balance while they run. The tail shape of *Smilodon* shows it attacked by pouncing from a hiding spot instead. *Smilodon* lived in packs with social structures.

Bones with healed injuries show that members of a pack cared for hurt *Smilodon*, allowing them to recover rather than letting them die from their injuries.

SLASHING TEETH

Smilodon had giant canine teeth that were shaped like saber swords. Saber-toothed cats had jaws that could open between 90 and 120 degrees. This allowed the cats to use their saber teeth to slash and stab their prey.

Drawings and models show what *Smilodon* may have looked like.

SPINOSAURUS

Spinosaurus was a large theropod that lived in what is now North Africa between 100 and 95 million years ago. It was probably semiaquatic. This means it lived on land but spent a good deal of time in water.

SAILS AND SWIMMING

Spinosaurus was likely the longest predatory dinosaur to ever live. It grew up to 50 feet (15 m) long and weighed about 14,000 pounds (6,350 kg). It had a large sail on its back and a crocodile-like jaw. In the late 2010s and early 2020s, researchers

Expeditions in the Moroccan desert between 2008 and 2019 uncovered many *Spinosaurus* fossils.

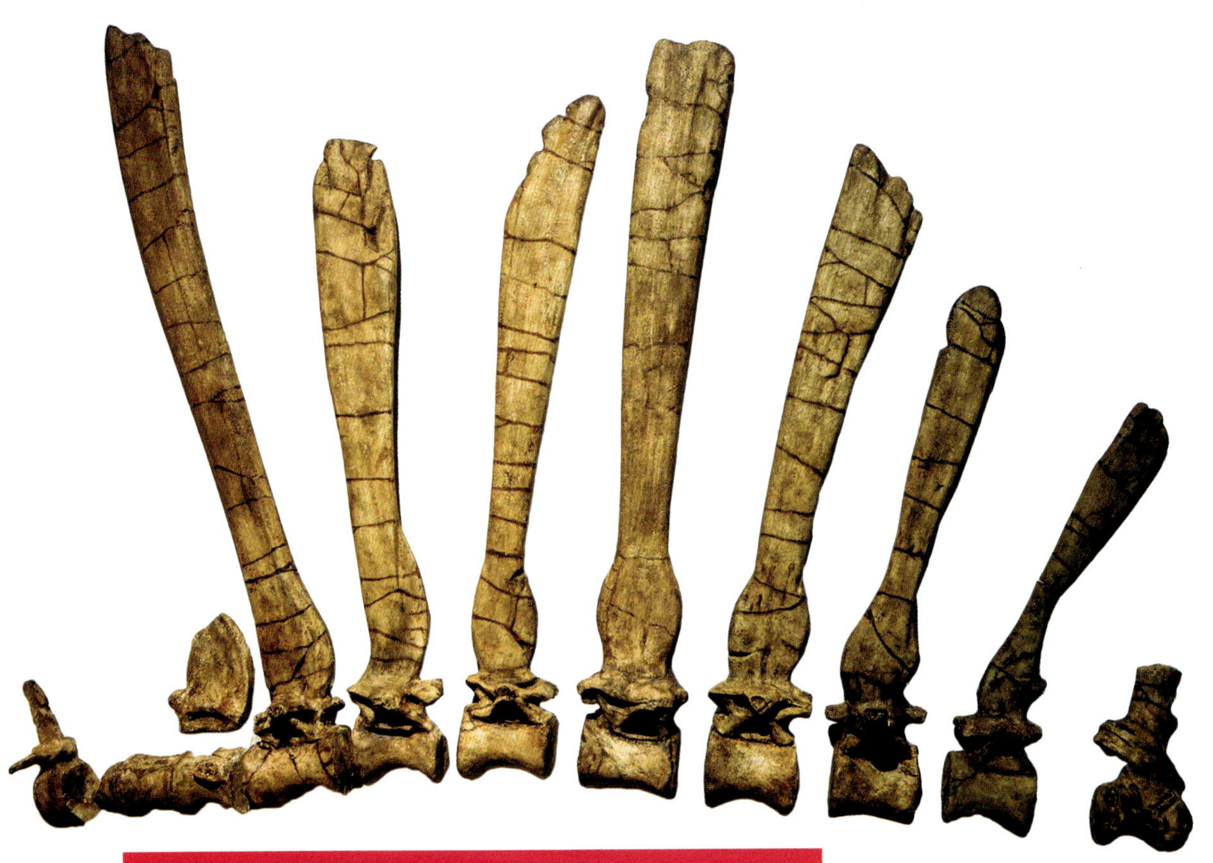

Scientists think *Spinosaurus* may have used its sail to attract a mate or regulate its body temperature.

worked to create a robotic model of the tail from fossilized bones. The model showed that the tail moved in a way that could propel the dinosaur through water. This is evidence that *Spinosaurus* could probably swim.

REDISCOVERED

In about 1910, the first skeletal remains of *Spinosaurus* were discovered in Egypt. They were displayed in a German museum. During World War II (1939–1945), bombs hit the museum and destroyed all the fossils. *Spinosaurus* fossils were not found again until 2008.

STEGOSAURUS

Stegosaurus was an armored herbivorous dinosaur. It lived 159 to 144 million years ago. *Stegosaurus* fossils have been excavated in Asia, Europe, and the United States. But it is still one of the rarest dinosaurs to discover. This is because *Stegosaurus* did not live in herds. It lived alone or in small groups.

The most complete *Stegosaurus* skeleton was found in 2022 near the town of Dinosaur, Colorado. It has 254 of about 320 bones. This *Stegosaurus*, nicknamed "Apex," is on display at the American Museum of Natural History. The museum filled any missing pieces of the skeleton with bones made by a 3D printer.

Apex was mounted with its spiked tail in the air, which scientists believe is how it stood to defend itself.

Stegosaurus had a brain about the size of a walnut.

LARGE BODY, SMALL BRAIN

Stegosaurus grew to about 30 feet (9 m) in length. It had bony, triangular plates on its back that stood upright. Some plates were more than 3 feet (1 m) tall. Their purpose is not clear. *Stegosaurus* used its spiked tail against predators. *Stegosaurus* had a very small head and brain for its size.

DID YOU KNOW?

Gary Larson created a cartoon about *Stegosaurus* for *The Far Side* comic series. In it, a caveman identifies the spiked tail of a *Stegosaurus* as a thagomizer. This was a word that Larson made up. But paleontologists have used *thagomizer* ever since.

Therizinosaurus claws were likely too weak to hold up to much pressure.

THERIZINOSAURUS

Therizinosaurus was a theropod with giant claws. It lived between 66 and 100 million years ago. The first *Therizinosaurus* remains were found in 1948 in the Gobi desert. At first, scientists thought *Therizinosaurus* was an ancestor of turtles. Fossils of its claws may have resembled the front arms of sea turtles. Later, researchers decided that the dinosaur was a theropod. Fossils showing the dinosaur's pubic bone and pelvis, along with toe bones similar to those of sauropods, may have led to this recategorization.

In 2000, an almost-complete *Therizinosaurus* skeleton was discovered in Utah. It was excavated in a desert location that was once an ancient seaway. The skeleton helped scientists fill in many gaps about this unusual dinosaur.

HERBIVORE

Therizinosaurus had a long, giraffe-like neck and small head. It grew to be about 33 feet (10 m) tall. Its long, curved claws resembled blades called scythes. They could be 3 feet (1 m) long. But the claws were likely not used for hunting. Based on the skeleton found in 2000, scientists think *Therizinosaurus* was a herbivore. Its claws helped gather vegetation.

Researchers have found some fossilized *Therizinosaurus* eggs.

TITANOBOA

Titanoboa was the largest snake to ever slither on Earth. It lived from 60 to 58 million years ago. In 2004, scientists began finding *Titanoboa* fossils at the Cerrejón coal mine in Colombia. This area was once a swampy jungle. Cerrejón provided rare access to fossils in a tropical location.

Most paleontologists hunt for fossils in open spaces such as deserts or in areas with exposed rocks. This is because it is very difficult to dig under trees and plants. But the Cerrejón miners

A life-size reconstruction of *Titanoboa* was displayed at Grand Central Terminal in New York City.

Researchers have uncovered several *Titanoboa* vertebrae.

had already removed all vegetation and dug deep into the earth. This gave researchers wide access to the fossils contained in the mine's layers of rock.

LARGEST EVER

So far, scientists have excavated fossils from at least 28 *Titanoboa* specimens. One nearly complete skeleton has been found with a skull. *Titanoboa* likely had more than 250 vertebrae. Based on the recovery of so many remains, the average length of this snake was likely about 42 feet (13 m). It weighed more than 2,500 pounds (1,130 kg). The longest snake alive today, the anaconda, grows to be about 20 feet (6 m) long.

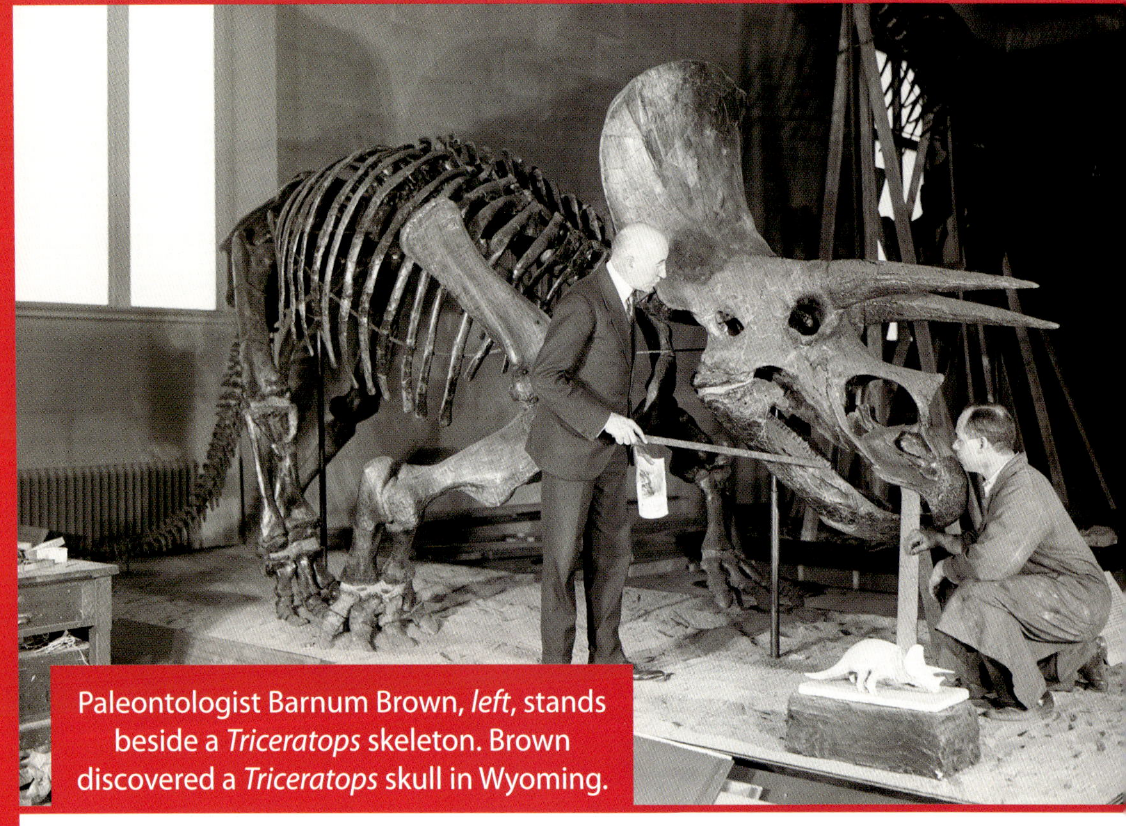

Paleontologist Barnum Brown, *left*, stands beside a *Triceratops* skeleton. Brown discovered a *Triceratops* skull in Wyoming.

TRICERATOPS

Triceratops was a herbivorous dinosaur that was about the size of a modern African elephant. It lived in the Late Cretaceous Period. Famed fossil hunter John Bell Hatcher found the first *Triceratops* skull in Wyoming in 1888. Since then, more than 50 skulls have been found in the western United States. A reconstructed *Triceratops* skeleton is on display at the Museums Victoria in Australia. Sometimes skeletons in museums are made of bones from multiple individuals, but 85 percent of the bones in this display are fossils from the same dinosaur.

HORNS AND FRILLS

Triceratops means "three-horned face." This refers to the horn on the dinosaur's snout and two horns above its eyes. A *Triceratops* skull could be up to 10 feet (3 m) long, including its frill. A frill is a bony extension of the skull. Scientists are still debating the purpose of this frill. Some think it helped *Triceratops* recognize the members of its species. Others think it was for display and mating.

Scientists agree that the *Triceratops* frill was not defensive armor.

TYRANNOSAURUS REX

Tyrannosaurus rex was one of the largest predators to ever roam the planet. It lived in what is now North America during the Cretaceous Period. Its name means "king of the tyrant lizards."

In 1902, paleontologist Barnum Brown discovered the first *T. rex* fossils in Montana. The most complete skeleton was found by paleontologist Sue Hendrickson in 1990. It has almost 90 percent of its bones. Hendrickson saw large vertebrae jutting from the side of a bluff in South Dakota. Six people

Tyrannosaurus rex made an appearance in many *Jurassic Park* movies, including the original.

Museum workers spent 30,000 hours preparing Sue's skeleton to be displayed.

spent 17 days digging out the fossils. This *T. rex* skeleton is now on display at the Field Museum in Chicago. It has been nicknamed "Sue" after Hendrickson.

IMPORTANT FIND

Scientists have learned a great deal from Sue. *T. rex* was an apex predator. It grew up to 40 feet (12 m) long and weighed up to about 19,555 pounds (8,870 kg). Its skull was 5 feet (1.5 m) long, and it had razor-sharp 6-inch (15 cm) teeth. *T. rex* also had the strongest bite of any land animal ever. However, it had very short arms for its size. Researchers have not found any fossils that reveal how the dinosaur used its arms.

Ursus spelaeus fossils were often preserved in the caves where they lived.

URSUS SPELAEUS

Ursus spelaeus is also known as the cave bear. It lived between 2.6 million and 11,700 years ago. The skeletal remains of more than 100,000 cave bears have been found in total. All were discovered in caves throughout Europe. The bones are so abundant that German soldiers boiled them for phosphates during World War I (1914–1918). In addition to skeletal remains, researchers have discovered trace fossils of claw marks and footprints.

ANCIENT DIETS

Male cave bears were similar in size to polar bears. Females were much smaller. The cave bear was an omnivore. Its diet consisted of mostly plants and seeds. But the bear sometimes ate meat. Scientists know this because they have found the bite marks of cave bears on the bones of other animals. Humans may have hunted cave bears.

U. spelaeus teeth help scientists understand the bear's diet.

VELOCIRAPTOR

Velociraptor was a carnivorous dinosaur that lived between 99 and 66 million years ago. The first *Velociraptor* fossils were discovered in the Gobi desert in 1923. Since then, more remains have been found in Asia. These include the famous skeletons of a *Velociraptor* and a *Protoceratops* fighting.

TURKEY-SIZED DINOSAUR

Velociraptor was about the size of a turkey. It had a long tail and feathers covering its body, including its wing-like arms. But it could not fly.

At least one complete *Velociraptor* skeleton with its skull has been found.

Scientists did not know *Velociraptor* had feathers until 2007.

Velociraptor had a long snout with 80 curved teeth. Its teeth were sharp and serrated. Its best-known feature is the large, curved claw on each foot. The claw was used for trapping and stabbing prey.

VELOCIRAPTOR MISUNDERSTOOD

Velociraptor was featured in Michael Crichton's book *Jurassic Park* and in movies based on the book. But Crichton's *Velociraptor* is much too large and has no feathers. There is also no evidence that *Velociraptor* hunted in packs or could have opened doors. These are both features of the *Velociraptor* in *Jurassic Park*. In real life, *Velociraptor* was probably as smart as an average bird.

GLOSSARY

crust
In geology, the outer layer of Earth, which is made of rock and minerals.

crustacean
A typically aquatic invertebrate with an exoskeleton and two pairs of antennae.

deposit
A natural collection of a material, often formed by natural processes.

efficient
Productive without wasting time or resources.

embalm
To protect a dead body from decay.

embryo
An organism in the early developmental stage in the womb or in an egg.

frond
A large leaf, often with smaller leaflets.

fungi
A kingdom of organisms that reproduce through spores and lack chlorophyll, including mushrooms and molds.

genus
A taxonomy category more specific than family but less specific than species.

invertebrate
An animal without a spinal column.

marine
Related to the sea.

order
A taxonomy category more specific than class but less specific than family.

organic
Related to living things.

quarry
An open-pit mine.

scavenger
An organism that consumes dead animals that it did not kill.

serrated
Having a notched or toothed edge.

tissue
A collection of cells that work together, forming the structure of a plant or animal.

vertebrate
An animal with a spinal column and a brain that is part of its nervous system.

whorl
A circular arrangement of parts, such as teeth or leaves, around a center point.

TO LEARN MORE

FURTHER READINGS

Johnson-Ransom, Evan. *Dinosaur World: Over 1,200 Amazing Dinosaurs, Famous Fossils, and the Latest Discoveries from the Prehistoric Era*. Appleseed, 2023.

Lomax, Dean R. *My Book of Fossils*. DK, 2022.

Lusted, Marcia Amidon. *Fossils, Rocks, and Minerals*. Abdo, 2022.

ONLINE RESOURCES

To learn more about fossils, please visit **abdobooklinks.com** or scan this QR code. These links are routinely monitored and updated to provide the most current information available.

INDEX

PHOTO CREDITS

Cover Photos: Shutterstock Images, front (ammonites, *Plesiosaurus*, nummulites, trilobites, *Phorusrhacos*, *Tyrannosaurus rex*), back (*Diplodocus*, *Calamites*); Barbara Ash/Shutterstock Images, front (*Mosasaurus*); Mark Kostich/Shutterstock Images, front (*Otodus megalodon*); Ronald Wilfred Jansen/Shutterstock Images, front (sponges); Puwadol Jaturawutthichai/Shutterstock Images, front (*Australopithecus*); David Herraez Calzada/Shutterstock Images, back (*Triceratops*)

Interior Photos: Shutterstock Images, 1, 5, 9, 17 (bottom), 18–19, 21, 25, 28–29, 31, 32–33, 38, 39, 47, 48–49, 56–57 (left), 56–57 (right), 59, 62, 62–63, 66–67, 70, 74–75, 80, 94, 94–95, 97, 100–101, 106–107, 112, 114, 135, 136–137, 139, 144, 147, 148, 160, 161, 170, 171, 177, 187; Manfred Ruckszio/Shutterstock Images, 3, 40; Visual China Group/Getty Images, 6; Bjoern Wylezich/Shutterstock Images, 8; Moha El-Jaw/Shutterstock Images, 10; Red Line Editorial, 11; Phil Degginger/Science Source, 12; Francois Gohier/VWPics/Universal Images Group/Getty Images, 13; Gilles Martin/Gamma-Rapho/Getty Images, 14; Patrick Aventurier/Gamma-Rapho/Getty Images, 15; Andriy Kananovych/Shutterstock Images, 16; Markus Matzel/ullstein bild/Getty Images, 17 (top); Steve Gschmeissner/Science Source, 20; PB/YB/Alamy, 22, 48, 50–51; Bridgette James/De Agostini Picture Library/Getty Images, 23; Kristen Grace/Florida Museum, 24; Barbara Strnadova/Science Source, 26; Francois Gohier/Science Source, 27, 116, 117, 134; The Natural History Museum, London/Science Source, 28, 32, 34, 37, 45, 46, 65, 71, 72–73, 81, 85, 141, 165, 184; Sophie Leguil/Shutterstock Images, 30–31; De Agostini Picture Library/Getty Images, 35, 55, 79, 93, 104–105, 185; William E. Fehr/Shutterstock Images, 36–37; Ana Dracaena/Shutterstock Images, 41; Paul Tafforeau/ESRF/Pascal Goetgheluck/Science Source, 42; Colin Keates/Dorling Kindersley/Science Source, 43; Mark Boulton/Science Source, 44–45; Breck P. Kent/Shutterstock Images, 52; Emma Jones/Shutterstock Images, 53; Han Zeng/Smithsonian, 54; Wikimedia Commons, 60, 92, 107, 121, 132–133, 142–143; Ondrej Michalek/Shutterstock Images, 61; Axel Jahnke/Shutterstock Images, 64; Pascal Goetgheluck/Science Source, 66, 103; John A. Anderson/Shutterstock Images, 68–69; Ronald Wilfred Jansen/Shutterstock Images, 69; Joe Belanger/Shutterstock Images, 73; Education Images/Universal Images Group/Getty Images, 74, 118, 140; Millard H. Sharp/Science Source, 76, 88, 127, 130–131, 179, 186; Insights/Universal Images Group/Getty Images, 77; Kelly van Dellen/Shutterstock Images, 78; Lida Xing, Edward L. Stanley, Ming Bai, and David C. Blackburn/Scientific Reports, 82–83; Field Museum Library/Premium Archive/Getty Images, 84; Doug Perrine/Nature Picture Library/Alamy, 86; Hypersphere/Science Source, 86–87; ullstein bild Dtl./Getty Images, 89; Rebel Red Runner/Shutterstock Images, 90; Wild Horizons/Universal Images Group/Getty Images, 91; Charlotte Bleijenberg/Shutterstock Images, 96–97; Ethan Miller/Getty Images News/Getty Images, 98; Mark Kostich/Shutterstock Images, 99; Javier Gonzalez Toledo/AFP/Getty Images, 101; Chris Ison/PA Images/Getty Images, 102; Kelvin Aitken/VWPics/AP Images, 105; Corbin17/Alamy, 108–109; Photo Researchers/Science History Images/Alamy, 109; Dotted Zebra/Alamy, 110–111; FPG/Hulton Archive/Archive Photos/Getty Images, 113; Jon G. Fuller/VWPics/Universal Images Group/Getty Images, 115; Andreas Gebert/dpa/picture alliance/Getty Images, 119; Dorling Kindersley/Science Source, 120; Puwadol Jaturawutthichai/Shutterstock Images, 122; Dave Einsel/Getty Images News/Getty Images, 123 (top); Michael Nicholson/Corbis Historical/Getty Images, 123 (bottom); Album/Prisma/Science Source, 124; Elmer Riggs/Field Museum Library/Premium Archive/Getty Images, 125; Jon G. Fuller/VWPics/Alamy, 126; Danny Ye/Shutterstock Images, 128–129, 146, 157, 166–167; Daniel Eskridge/Shutterstock Images, 129; Dave Buresh/Denver Post/Getty Images, 130; Mark Turner/Alamy, 133; James Nielsen/Houston Chronicle/Hearst Newspapers/Getty Images, 136; William Vanderson/Fox Photos/Hulton Archive/Getty Images, 138; Lisa Maree Williams/Getty Images News/Getty Images, 145 (top); Independent Picture Service/Universal Images Group/Getty Images, 145 (bottom); Grégoire Campione/AFP/Getty Images, 149; Paul D. Stewart/Science Source, 150; Martin Bache/Alamy, 151; Mark Brandon/Shutterstock Images, 152; Spencer Platt/Getty Images News/Getty Images, 153; Lucas Oleniuk/Toronto Star/Getty Images, 154, 155, 158; Holger Hollemann/dpa/picture alliance/Getty Images, 156; Matthew Dicker/Shutterstock Images, 159; Bone Clones, Inc./Science Source, 162; Melnikov Dmitriy/Shutterstock Images, 163; Jaroslav Moravcik/Shutterstock Images, 164; Eugen Thome/Shutterstock Images, 167; Akkharat Jarusilawong/Shutterstock Images, 168; Sergey Krasovskiy/Stocktrek Images/Science Source, 168–169; Josep Lago/AFP/Getty Images, 172; Bill O'Leary/The Washington Post/Getty Images, 173; Lev Radin/Pacific Press/LightRocket/Getty Images, 174–175; Thierry Monasse/Getty Images News/Getty Images, 175; Corey Ford/Stocktrek Images/Science Source, 176; Michael Loccisano/Getty Images Entertainment/Getty Images, 178–179; Bettmann/Getty Images, 180; David Herraez Calzada/Shutterstock Images, 181; Murray Close/Moviepix/Getty Images, 182; Mark Wilson/Newsmakers/Hulton Archive/Getty Images, 183

ABDOBOOKS.COM
Published by Abdo Reference, a division of ABDO, PO Box 398166, Minneapolis, Minnesota 55439.

Printed in China.
082025
012026

Editor: Marley Richmond
Series Designer: Colleen McLaren
Production Designer: Ebonee Estrella

LIBRARY OF CONGRESS CONTROL NUMBER: 2025939301

PUBLISHER'S CATALOGING-IN-PUBLICATION DATA
Names: Herman, Miles, author.
Title: The fossil encyclopedia / by Miles Herman
Description: Minneapolis, Minnesota: Abdo Reference, 2026 | Series: Geology encyclopedias | Includes online resources and index.
Identifiers: ISBN 9781098298890 (lib. bdg.) | ISBN 9798384932697 (ebook)
Subjects: LCSH: Fossils--Juvenile literature. | Fossilogy--Juvenile literature. | Paleontology--Juvenile literature. | Rocks--Juvenile literature. | Geology--Juvenile literature. | Encyclopedias--Juvenile literature.
Classification: DDC 560--dc23